REPENTANCE
THE GOOD NEWS

OSILAMA OSIME

WESTBOW
PRESS®
A DIVISION OF THOMAS NELSON
& ZONDERVAN

WestBow Press books may be ordered through booksellers or by contacting:

WestBow Press
A Division of Thomas Nelson & Zondervan
1663 Liberty Drive
Bloomington, IN 47403
www.westbowpress.com
844-714-3454

Because of the dynamic nature of the Internet, any web addresses or
links contained in this book may have changed since publication and
may no longer be valid. The views expressed in this work are solely those
of the author and do not necessarily reflect the views of the publisher,
and the publisher hereby disclaims any responsibility for them.

Any people depicted in stock imagery provided by Getty Images are
models, and such images are being used for illustrative purposes only.
Certain stock imagery © Getty Images.

The Christian Standard Bible. Copyright © 2017 by Holman Bible Publishers.
Used by permission. Christian Standard Bible®, and CSB® are federally
registered trademarks of Holman Bible Publishers, all rights reserved.

ISBN: 978-1-6642-6281-2 (sc)
ISBN: 978-1-6642-6279-9 (hc)
ISBN: 978-1-6642-6280-5 (e)

Library of Congress Control Number: 2022906296

Print information available on the last page.

WestBow Press rev. date: 04/26/2022

To my parents,
Evangelist Marcel Momodu "M.M." Osime
and Madam Mary Azimeguere Magoh,

and to Apostle Patrick A. A. Egabor, Ambassador for Christ

CONTENTS

PREFACE

Repentance when we offend one another may not be necessary and essential in our forgiving each other. However, seeking God's forgiveness through repenting of our sins is a crucial ingredient to salvation and reconciliation with God in the hereafter and afterlife. We are all sinners, and both John the Baptist, the harbinger, and Jesus the Christ preached repentance as the Good News.

It is undeniable that true followers of the Christian faith have signs that cause them to stand out in a crowd. The Gospel of John reports the ease with which Peter Simon was identified as one of the disciples of Jesus Christ even when he chose to pass incognito (18:15–26). And in the Gospel of Mark, while issuing the Great Commission, Jesus spoke of the signs that will follow those who believe. However, the gifts of prophecy, speaking in tongues, laying of hands, and healing the sick, and performing miracles in His name are not evidence nor guarantee of salvation in the life after this life.

When the disciples asked Jesus to increase their faith, He told them all they needed to move mountains was faith as little as a mustard seed. He went further to add:

> "Which one of you having a servant tending sheep
> or plowing will say to him when he comes in from
> the field, 'Come at once and sit down to eat'?
> Instead, will he not tell him, 'Prepare something

for me to eat, get ready, and serve me while I eat and drink; later you can eat and drink'? Does he thank that servant because he did what was commanded? In the same way, **when you have done all that you were commanded,** you should say, '**We are unworthy servants;** we've only done our duty.'" (Luke 17:7–10 CSB; emphasis mine)

When you have done all that you were commanded to do, do not forget that you are *unworthy*—a significant reminder that the tool or implement has no claim to the harvest. There are signs that follow the servant of a master. But no matter how efficient and effective the servant is, the servant has no claim to the harvest. Jesus cautioned His disciples to keep in mind that they remain unworthy even after they have done their duty.

A book of this length cannot attempt to exhaustively discuss the subjects of evil and sin, repentance and forgiveness, and grace. But it seeks to point to the fact that repentance is the crucial second pillar of the narrow gate of salvation, along with belief in Christ Jesus as the Son of God. It doubles as the bridge, the only factor that brings us back to God. The availability of repentance to mankind is clear manifestation of God's grace. Under the law, disobedience attracted a curse:

> For all who rely on the works of the law are under a curse, because it is written, Everyone who does not do everything written in the book of the law is cursed. (Galatians 3:10 CSB)

However, with the Gospel of Christ, there is the offer of an opportunity to repent and obtain forgiveness for all violations. When He sent His disciples out in pairs, they went and preached repentance. When He was ready to ascend, He restated the same instructions.

So they went out and preached that people should repent. (Mark 6:12 CSB)

He also said to them, "This is what is written: The Messiah will suffer and rise from the dead the third day, and **repentance for forgiveness of sins** will be proclaimed in his name to all the nations, beginning at Jerusalem." (Luke 24:46–47 CSB; emphasis mine)

The theme of repentance runs through all the books of the Bible, from Genesis through Revelation, but references will be limited to a few that are most relevant to the point that repenting of our sins is a significant pillar to salvation.

I hope the issues raised stimulate the reader to search the scriptures for themselves. Salvation is a personal concern and cannot be attained through the doctrines of any denomination or creed. Hence a personal understanding is mandatory. If you find the time to go through this book, I encourage you to disagree with the conclusions reached, but in doing so, search the scriptures for yourself and formulate a position that will reconcile you with your Creator.

My appreciation goes to my brothers, Dr. William Hill and Prof. Michael Ikhariale, who took time to review the initial manuscript and made invaluable suggestions. I thank God for the love and affections of my wife, Catherine, and my grandchildren, Micah, Elizabeth (TiTi), Isabella, Zoe (Odetho), and Eshiemokhai. Their support in this work is immeasurable.

CHAPTER 1

"GO AND SIN NO MORE":
A SIGNIFICANT CONDITION FOR SALVATION

There is a growing selective obliteration of the truth of the Word of God. However, the truth must still prevail in an era when the scriptures are under siege by those masquerading as men and women of God who lay claim to proclaiming God's Word. Evangelism that should proclaim the Good News of the Gospel is now a soothsaying, prophecy-only business. Revelations from an unchangeable God are reversed as quickly as they are declared. When these self-serving "evangelicals" care to reference the scripture, half-truths and misrepresentation of the Word are declared. The message delivered after allegedly hearing from the unchangeable God is flip-flopped, and shame and ridicule are brought on the faithful.

"We of the earthly church of grace of God believe that sin cannot keep us from God's grace" seems to be the prevalent declaration. The supporting argument goes like this: our God is faithful, merciful, and gracious. His only begotten Son, Jesus Christ, said to come unto Him just as you are. We proceed to look the other way while a racist, homophobic, xenophobic, pathologic liar and megalomaniac stumbles into leadership and camouflages himself as the champion of Christianity. Evangelicals take a break

1

from evangelizing and preaching the Word but fall over themselves to prophesy that the savior is here—a crusader for Christian values who cannot find Genesis in the Bible. When evangelicals are unable to boldly preach against hatred, the church and the Gospel of Christ are severely compromised.

When the world looks to professional politicians to preach on honesty, unity, integrity, and love for our neighbors, while evangelism is focused on pandering falsehood as God's prophecy, the salt that has no taste is a sweet metaphor. The quackery of masquerading as God's prophets damages the spiritual standing and integrity of so-called "evangelicals" as false prophecy misrepresents God. As columnist Mike Ikhariale has observed, "Falsehood, as an ethical delict, whether from the political soapbox or from a religious pulpit does have long-lasting integrity and reputational consequences."[1]

Spreading the Good News of the Gospel as outright falsehoods, half-truths, or misrepresentations has consequences beyond here and now. Numbers 22:22–35 is a sufficient reminder that God can raise donkeys if the prophets will not be obedient and speak the truth to power. Today, our prophets will not even change their false prophecy when it is shown outright to be not of God. Balaam repented when the donkey spoke.

> Balaam said to the angel of the Lord, "I have sinned, for I did not know that you were standing in the path to confront me. And now, if it is evil in your sight, I will go back." (Numbers 22:34 CSB)

Our modern-day diviners and prophet wannabes will continue declaring their false visions from God in the face of reality that is acknowledged and declared by other human beings with an

---

[1] Mike Ikhariale, "Donald Trump and His Nigerian 'YouTube' Fake Prophets," *Independent* (January 20, 2021), accessed January 26, 2021, https:// independent.ng/donald-trump-and-his-nigerian-youtube-fake-prophets.

overwhelming majority. God is not mocked. History has recorded that colonization and slavery rode on the back of evangelism. In the year of our Lord 2020, evangelists were sponsoring racism, superior race, demagoguery, and tribalism, with angels of God seen traveling the globe and invalidating national election votes cast by lesser citizens. Evangelists, instead of preaching the Good News of salvation, took to the pulpit to prophesy that God is sending an army of voting angels transcontinental to flip an election in favor of a loser. We seem to be more concerned with revealing to the uninformed that God speaks to and through us. Our ignorance of the third commandment is, however, put in public display.

> Do not misuse the name of the Lord your God, because the Lord will not leave anyone unpunished who misuses his name. (Exodus 20:7 CSB)

The political intent of such prophecies is not hidden, and that the name of Holy God is being exploited to drive a political agenda is obvious.

The word of the Lord through the prophet Ezekiel to the shepherds of God's flock is a pertinent and good reference. God will demand the flock from the shepherds, and there are consequences for engaging in a culture war instead of feeding the flock.

> This is what the Lord God says: Look, I am against the shepherds. I will demand my flock from them and prevent them from shepherding the flock. The shepherds will no longer feed themselves, for I will rescue my flock from their mouths so that they will not be food for them. (Ezekiel 34:10 CSB)

As Ikhariale has noted, "Over the centuries, white racist Christians have misinterpreted the Bible to justify their criminal humiliation of fellow human beings through slavery, colonialism, racism, apartheid, and many other ungodly sociopolitical policies."[2] When will racist Christians get it right? Is it when God resorts to speaking through donkeys again? Or after He raises stones to praise Him? Or when He institutes alternative means of rescuing His flock from the mouths of the shepherds? Does God's Word promise to heal and restore the land before we repent and return to Him—or the other way round?

Who can dispute the truth that Jesus invited us to come to Him without conditions? "Come to me, all of you who are weary and burdened, and I will give you rest," says Matthew 11:28 (CSB).

However, there is a second half to this truth that is obliterated or kept mute. When we encounter Christ, we "go and sin no more." The grace of God forbids us to remain in sin. The grace of God draws us to repentance. The Gospel of John narrates the story of the woman caught in adultery. Although lawyers were not called in this case, the prosecutors abandoned their case without calling witnesses. The defendant and accused was caught in the act. Even she will witness against herself. Judge Jesus, just and diligent, stooped and maybe recorded the case presented. Then He asked an opening question of the prosecutors. "Has any one of you here never sinned?" And I suppose He returned to taking more notes. Diligence! This was a serious matter; someone's life was at stake. By the time He looked up from His notes again, the prosecutors had all left His presence. Short case. Verdict: not guilty. However, the acquittal was on condition: "Go and sin no more."

> Then the scribes and the Pharisees brought a
> woman caught in adultery, making her stand in the

---

[2] Ikhariale, "Donald Trump."

4

center. "Teacher," they said to him, "this woman was caught in the act of committing adultery. In the law Moses commanded us to stone such women. So what do you say?" They asked this to trap him, in order that they might have evidence to accuse him. Jesus stooped down and started writing on the ground with his finger. When they persisted in questioning him, he stood up and said to them, "The one without sin among you should be the first to throw a stone at her." Then he stooped down again and continued writing on the ground. When they heard this, they left one by one, starting with the older men. Only he was left, with the woman in the center. When Jesus stood up, he said to her, "Woman, where are they? Has no one condemned you?" "No one, Lord," she answered. "Neither do I condemn you," said Jesus. **"Go, and from now on do not sin anymore."** (John 8:3–11 CSB; emphasis mine)

This translation says, "Go, and from now on do not..." This is the underlying requirement of grace: an imperative not to sin anymore. The struggle to live without sin is what we are called to as believers in Christ. While God's grace provides undeserved pardon for our transgressions, the Good News of the Gospel declares that there is forgiveness of sins when we repent. Believers in Christ are not called to be sinless but to sin *less*, and when they sin to seek forgiveness through repentance.

The rest of this book will search the scriptures concerning the subjects of forgiveness, repentance, and grace. Balaam acknowledged he had sinned. Are our evangelicals willing to start speaking only the Word that the Lord truly commands them to speak, or will they continue to engage in political campaigns from the pulpit?

CHAPTER 2

HINDRANCE TO OFFERING FORGIVENESS

From the Christian's perspective, forgiveness is a subject that is both crucial and critical. The Gospel recorders observed that Christ was questioned pointedly about it, and all who look to the Bible for an understanding of forgiveness, find it clearly taught and demonstrated in the life of Jesus Christ.

Before looking at why forgiveness is so important in the practice of Christianity, let us explore the factors that might hinder our willingness to forgive those who have offended us. Understanding our reluctance to forgive despite the demands made on us by the scriptures could provide us with a clearer path toward being able to forgive with ease.

There may be several reasons for withholding forgiveness; here are nine of the most common.

1. **Demanding reparation.** A belief in our right to demand reparation for damages suffered might come with an inherent reluctance to offer up forgiveness until such reparations are made.

2. **Ego.** An ego damaged or hurt may demand that we, the offended, keep a grudge against the offender as the minimum requirement to save face. We think, *How can I forgive them after what they have done to me?* It is

6

calculated that the offense has already cost so much that forgiving will only add to the damage. An unwillingness to forgive could be a defense mechanism to protect our injured ego.

3. **Hope of reconciliation.** When an offense is an act that violates trust, the risks involved in the restoration of confidence following such an act of betrayal become problematic. This hindrance to forgiveness seems to confuse forgiving others with reconciling with them. The statement "How can I forgive them after I have been so violated?" translates then to "How can I reconcile with them after I have been so violated"? When we are injured because of deception or misleading circumstances, the feeling that the pain was preventable might make forgiveness difficult.

4. **Score-settling.** In seeking to settle the score with the offender, it might not be problematic to resolve the issues related to a perceived offense or source of conflict. However, a strong desire to score an equalizing point drives unforgiveness. "An eye for an eye" is a biblical verse thrown out frequently to justify the need for vengeance before we can forgive. The offender or perpetrator is expected to experience some pain, suffering, or punishment commensurate in severity to the experience of the victim. There is lack of empathy towards the perpetrator of offense. The punishment is deserved and must not be mitigated. There is no "closure" until the perpetrator is convicted—or as Shakespeare's Shylock would have it, a "a pound…of flesh."

5. **Lack of awareness.** Depending on the injury inflicted, the victim may be unaware of the fact that they have been victimized or that a conflict or offense exists. The perpetrator in this circumstance may not feel need to

seek forgiveness. The guilt of such crimes torments the perpetrator regardless of their confession to anyone else.

6. **Self-righteousness.** A belief in the rightness of our ways can result in us being blind to the offenses, however small or large, which we can cause by our words or actions. This belief system assumes that we are always appropriate and right in all our interactions with others.

7. **Unrepentance.** An unwillingness on the part of the offender to express remorse and accept guilt, or an inability or reluctance to apologize, will almost certainly hinder the chances of receiving forgiveness.

8. **Denial.** Denying the facts of a traumatic event, minimizing severity of injury and pain caused, trivializing the deed, and generally pretending that what happened did not happen or that it happened differently can be attempts to justify the injury caused and to placate the injured.

9. **Habit or passivity.** Offensive behavior may be a pattern from the offender that is regularized when the victim is repeatedly subjected to abuse and neglect. The feeling of experiencing subjugation and rejection in silence could foster unforgiveness.

CHAPTER 3

WHAT IS FORGIVENESS?

Let me state upfront that forgiveness is a multifaceted idea. It can be given to us; we can extend it to others; we can even give it to ourselves. The act of forgiving involves giving up the pain, grudge, or anger emanating from or related to an offense. There is usually an offender and one who is offended, but the same person can both be the offender and the offended if they feel guilt for a situation, they believe they have been responsible for.

Psychologists agree that forgiveness involves relinquishing feelings of resentment and anger towards another person or group or letting go the need to seek revenge and settle scores with someone who has done us wrong.[3] It is the process of healing emotional pain or a wound, whether self-inflicted or inflicted by others. Therefore, forgiveness is therapeutic as we forgive others. Forgiveness is self-directed as the person who forgives is healed emotionally and is released from the remote control of the perpetrator. Forgiveness could but does not need to be triggered by the actions of others, for example, the expression of remorse and guilt by the offender or the promise of reparation or restitution.

What constitutes an offense warranting forgiveness or

---

[3] "What Is Forgiveness?", Greater Good Magazine, accessed January 26, 2022, https://greatergood.berkeley.edu/topic/forgiveness/definition.

vengeance is an individual matter. The spectrum of such issues ranges from someone not responding to our greetings to severely traumatic experiences. Unlike harm done to the physical body, injury to the emotions of a person can be assessed and expressed only by the offended. The healing of such emotional injury depends entirely on the offended and their willingness to forgive and to heal. As Desmond Tutu and Mpho Tutu wrote,

> Forgiveness feels as if a weight has been lifted off you and you are free and you are free to let go of the past and move forward in your life. It may not be found in a single act of grace or a single string of words, but rather in a process.[4]

It is relevant to point out that forgiveness does not mean denying the occurrence of an assault on our emotions, nor condoning, reframing, or validating incidents that upset our emotions. It also does not mean forgetting that the trauma happened nor minimizing the impact of trauma. "Forgive and forget" is an unrealistic expectation. You can forgive, but you cannot, in the absence of a memory pathology, forget a real-life trauma experience. A third-degree burn might heal, but the scars are not erased. A medical doctor who loses a confidante, best friend, and wife at age of thirty-six may heal emotionally, but forgetting the events of the trauma is not part of moving on.

True self-directed forgiveness is unconditional and does not solicit or expect a prize from the offender or anyone else. True forgiveness does not cajole a perceived offender into accepting guilt or wrongdoing. Walking up to a perceived offender to declare "I forgive you" is not true forgiveness. The person who is being forgiven may not even have memory of the offense for which he is

---

[4] Desmond Tutu and Mpho Tutu, *The Book of Forgiving: The Fourfold Path to Healing Ourselves and the World* (New York, Harper One: 2014), p. 54.

forgiven. The person offering this kind of forgiveness is more likely seeking to get some attention to disclose a perceived grievance.

Some distinction must be made between unconditional self-directed forgiveness and repentance-induced forgiveness. In self-directed forgiveness, the victim finds the grace to let go the cause of emotional pain for the sake of the healing that comes from self-restoration, freedom from stagnation at a point in life, wasted cognitive energy dissipated ruminating about the offending event and the perpetrator, and the incarceration of fear and anger. Repentance-induced forgiveness, on the other hand, opens the possibility of reconciliation, restoration, and reunion. It originates when an offender or perpetrator willingly accepts guilt, is remorseful for the injury caused, and unconditionally seeks forgiveness. Repentance-induced forgiveness requires the perpetrator to determine their guilt independently before moving forward to seek forgiveness.

Forgiveness is an affective (emotional) action, and as such, refusal to forgive others or forgive oneself results in an emotional disturbance, the types of which include anger, stress disorders, anxiety, and depression. Besides emotional disorders, psychiatrists and psychologists recognize behavioral and cognitive disorders. Unlike behavioral and cognitive disorders, most affective disorders can be resolved through counseling therapy. Forgiveness is a significant component of effective counseling towards healing the self of emotional pain, conflict, or crisis. The anger of unforgiveness incarcerates and is emotionally debilitating.

In *The Book of Forgiving*, Tutu and Tutu clearly delineate two divergent natural responses consequent to suffering physical, emotional, or psychosocial injury from others. The one response draws us into a revenge cycle of seeking retaliation and inflicting similar pain on our offender. This is a closed loop in which one step inevitably generates the next. Inflicting a retaliatory injury on our offender does not heal the injury inflicted. Unforgiveness fuels and sustains the activities of the revenge cycle, which succeeds when there is stagnation in our life at the point of injury.

The alternative response to revenge and unforgiveness is what Tutu and Tutu call the Fourfold Path of Forgiveness, which heals and releases us from the pain and burden of our injury and draws us toward forgiveness, which they characterize as "a universal and nonsectarian cycle." Forgiveness charts a course that releases us from the stagnation at the point of injury and propels us into freedom and a new life defined by us and not defined by our offender. It does not require faith, but belief in the Gospel of Christ makes the process easier.

Forgiveness does not condone an act. Forgiveness does not release the offender of responsibility for their actions, it does not erase accountability, and it is not about turning a blind eye or even turning the other cheek. It is not about letting someone off the hook or condoning a monstrous act. Forgiveness is simply about understanding that every one of us is "both inherently good and inherently flawed."[5] In forgiveness there is mercy for the offended and the offender. Whenever we are emotionally hurt or offended, we are challenged either to seek revenge before moving on or to move past the offense without retaliation. We are faced with making a choice between forgiving and revenging. There is a lag time between the point of emotional injury, when we feel upset, angry, disappointed, and sad, and the point when we initiate revenge or retaliation or decide to forgive. This time between the injury and the action we initiate to respond, whether in the form of forgiveness or retaliation, could be many hours or days, or it could be immediate.

The scriptures have two accounts when this response time was immediate. First was at the Cross, when Jesus pleaded for the forgiveness of those actively in the process of falsely accusing, persecuting, and hanging Him. Next was when Stephen pleaded

---

[5] Tutu and Tutu, p. 57.

for forgiveness for those who were still in the process of stoning him to death.

The time from traumatic experience to entering either the revenge cycle or forgiveness path varies from person to person, according to the individual's vulnerability and speed in navigating the stages of grief—unbelief or denial that the offending act happened, feelings of disappointment that the offense occurred, and coming to terms with the reality of the pain or injury caused.

Tutu and Tutu outline the four steps of the Fourfold Path of Forgiveness:[6]

1. **Telling the story.** This requires acknowledging the facts of what happened, the truth as it happened and was perceived. This recounting could be made to others such as spiritual leaders or a therapist—someone capable of providing a safe space and keeping the trust of information disclosed in confidence. You could also tell the story to yourself or to God in prayer. Recounting the truth of what happened to yourself is most important. Where and how the narration occurs are secondary to acknowledging the facts of what happened and accepting that what happened cannot be undone. Whatever happened is yesterday and behind. Whatever happened may have left marks or memory scars, but the events cannot be changed. "Do not worry too much about how or where you tell your story. What is most important to healing is that you tell your story."[7]

2. **Naming the Hurt.** Yes, it hurts. Where does it hurt, and what is the nature of the pain? What feelings did the offending incident induce that make you feel uncomfortable? When we can clearly state what offended

---

[6] Tutu and Tutu, pp. 67–162.
[7] Tutu and Tutu, p. 87.

us and how and are able to identify the nature of emotional pain caused, then we have come to a place where we can accept the truth of the past and move past it. It is not realistic to claim that we had no feeling following an event that hurt us emotionally. Such claim is avoidant and establishes the mindset for revenge. If you were hurt and know it, instead of seeking revenge, identify the injury and name the pain. These are crucial to healing.

3. **Granting forgiveness.** Granting forgiveness is how we move forward along the fourfold path. When we choose to forgive, we are positioned to start a new page in life that has no record of the pain and grief of the past hurt. Most important, the grip of the person who has hurt us is loosened. While the events cannot be undone, the painful memory of the perpetrator are erased. Granting forgiveness releases us from being stuck in time at the point where we were injured. It moves us pass the point where, like a scratched record, our thoughts repeat over and over the events that hurt. The events are rehearsed and ruminated upon, and the presence of the perpetrator is always large and overbearing.

When we grant forgiveness, this cycle of reliving the painful event is broken, and we are released from the bondage of the constant presence of the perpetrator in our thoughts. Tutu and Tutu put it this way:

> We choose forgiveness because it is how we find freedom and keep from remaining trapped in an endless loop of telling our story and naming our hurts. It is how we move from victim to hero. A victim is in a position of weakness and subject to the whims of others. Heroes are people who determine their own fate and their own future. A

> victim has nothing to give and no choices to make. A hero has the strength and ability to be generous and forgiving, and the power and freedom that come from being able to make the choice to grant forgiveness.[8]

Forgiveness enables us to recall the traumatic incident from a position of power, free from the intimidation of the perpetrator. The events become a new story—a story of forgiveness, empowerment, and freedom.

Granting forgiveness to others is enhanced when we focus on the substance of what is hurtful rather than on the person of the offender. What was it that exactly happened? What and where is the difference in opinion? If someone we have chosen to be a friend offends us, there is a point of separation in values, thoughts, or behavior that results in offense. If we focus on what happened that is offensive, the cause of conflict, it might be easier to grant forgiveness. When we begin to separate our friend from their obnoxious actions, then we are positioned to grapple with these offensive acts, to resolve them and break the cycle that holds us down. T. D. Jakes puts it this way: "In order to begin this process, we must see the issue, and not the individual, as the enemy. It is the conflict we want to resolve and not the person we want to defeat."[9]

4. **Renewing or releasing the relationship.** Before or after an offensive act, a relationship exists between the offended and the offender. Even when it is the offensive act that brought them together for the first time, the offense initiates a relationship that is "created and maintained by the very act of harm that stands between

---

[8] Tutu and Tutu, pp. 121–122.
[9] T. D. Jakes, *Let It Go: Forgive So You Can Be Forgiven*, (New York: First Atria, 2013), p. 67.

you. This relationship, like every relationship that calls for forgiveness, must be either renewed or released."[10]

Renewing a relationship that was hurtful is not restoring the past relationship but creating a new relationship that is different and draws from the experience of the offensive injurious act. On the other hand, there is need to release and let go of a relationship when safety issues are involved, and we are at continued risk of being hurt. Releasing a relationship frees us from continued trauma and victimhood and from letting an occurrence and a perpetrator take hold of our mind. It brings an end to ruminating about the person and the events that hurt.

In addition to the therapeutic and healing effect, forgiveness is also the second major pillar of salvation for people of faith. Jesus Christ gave guidance on how many times we must forgive those that offend us, taught that we must not approach the altar with our offerings if we were yet to forgive our brother, told a detailed parable on the restoration of a forgiven son, and when asked to give a prayer sample inserted our need to forgive others.

Consistent with His teaching, Jesus set the standard for self-directed forgiveness when He spontaneously offered forgiveness to those who had betrayed Him, falsely accused and charged Him, flogged Him, and stripped Him of His clothes and hung Him on a cross. While His accusers were yet celebrating the perpetration of injustice on an innocent person, the "victim" pleaded for forgiveness for those hurting Him:

> Then Jesus said, "Father, forgive them, because they do not know what they are doing." (Luke 23:34a CSB)

---

[10] Tutu and Tutu, p. 54.

Even as they tortured and executed Him, He prayed for forgiveness for His executioners who went on to draw lots over His garments. The grace of forgiveness was perfected.

Jesus, of course, knew He had to prepare Himself and continue to be free from sin. Who is the human who will not be hurt when betrayed, falsely accused and charged, and sent to be executed? The anger and emotional pain that confronted Jesus immediately before His death may well have been His final temptation. He chose not to go down with the baggage of anger or a grudge against anyone. He healed Himself of the emotional injury inflicted just at the point of death. He forgave.

The first martyr of Christendom took a leaf from Jesus. Stephen, described in Acts 6:5 as "a man full of faith and the Holy Spirit," was falsely accused of blasphemy against Moses and God. Bold, defiant, and full of courage, Stephen delivered a sermon recorded in Acts 7 in which he concluded that his accusers were resisting the Holy Spirit as their ancestors had, remaining stiff-necked and unrepentant. His courage and boldness in pointing out his accusers' pattern of persecuting, betraying, and killing prophets, including the crucifixion of the Messiah, enraged them. They rushed at him, dragged him out of the city, and started stoning him. While they were stoning him, he prayed for their forgiveness.

> They yelled at the top of their voices, covered their ears, and together rushed against him. They dragged him out of the city and began to stone him. And the witnesses laid their garments at the feet of a young man named Saul. While they were stoning Stephen, he called out, "Lord Jesus, receive my spirit!" He knelt down and cried out with a loud voice, "Lord, do not hold this sin against them!" And after saying this, he fell asleep. (Acts 7:57–60 CSB)

The balm to emotional injury is forgiveness. Jesus and Stephen applied this balm as first aid when the injury was fresh and raw. The treatment of emotional injury with the ointment of forgiveness is just as effective when applied to old wounds. Who has offended and emotionally injured you? Forgiveness will heal you.

Our unwillingness to forgive others offends God. Jesus illustrates this with the parable of the unforgiving servant recorded in Matthew 18:23–35. This parable tells of a master who showed compassion on a servant and forgave the servant's indebtedness to the tune of ten thousand talents. However, when this same servant encountered a fellow servant who owed him just a hundred talents, he would not grant forgiveness. The fellow servant begged to be given an extension of the payment due date. The servant who had been granted forgiveness of his own debts instead had his colleague thrown in jail until full payment was made of what was owed. The master was disappointed that the person to whom he had just shown forgiveness would not forgive another.

> "You wicked servant! I forgave you all that debt because you begged me. Shouldn't you also have had mercy on your fellow servant, as I had mercy on you?" (Matthew 18:32–33 CSB)

Forgiveness entails mercy towards the offender. Unbelievable!

The conclusion of the parable declares that as the master dealt harshly with his unforgiving servant, "so also my heavenly Father will do to you unless every one of you forgives his brother or sister from your heart" (Matthew 18:35 CSB). Our not forgiving one another sincerely ("from your heart") displeases God.

Jesus had a way of answering questions posed to him beyond the extent of the question. He would respond with parables that covered the literal interpretation and the unspoken intent of the question. The parable of the unforgiving servant was told in response to a question by the apostle Simon Peter, who asked,

"Lord, how many times shall I forgive my brother or sister who sins against me? As many as seven times?" (Matthew 18:21 CSB). How many times will you seek a doctor's treatment for an injury to your limbs or internal organs? How many times will you seek treatment for a concussion, for a gastrointestinal problem, for a genitourinary problem? How many times do we seek treatment when we are physically injured or fall sick? Seven times? Or "seventy times seven" times (Matthew18:22)? Maybe every time! I suppose Peter got a number for an answer because he suggested a number.

Unforgiveness hinders healing of emotional injury and pain; it sustains a traumatic experience through daily rehashing of the events of the injury, causing us to re-experience the offense. The offender moves on, but the offended is stagnated and repeatedly self-reinflicts with the memory of the painful incidence. Forgiveness does not imply that we have no cause to be offended nor that it was right that we were trampled on. The inability to express anger at an offensive behavior is not Christlike. Anger should be acknowledged and expressed. However, once appropriately expressed towards an offense, it should be let go and not sustained and nursed. Paul addresses this in chapter four of his letter to the Ephesians:

> **Be angry and do not sin. Don't let the sun go down on your anger**, and don't give the devil an opportunity. (Ephesians 4:26–27 CSB; emphasis mine)

> Let all bitterness, anger and wrath, shouting and slander be removed from you, along with all malice. And be kind and compassionate to one another, forgiving one another, just as God also forgave you in Christ. (Ephesians 4:31–32 CSB)

CHAPTER 4

REPENTANCE-INDUCED FORGIVENESS

Forgive us our trespasses, as we forgive those that
trespass against us. (Matthew 6: 12 CSB)

The word "forgive" is used twice in the Lord's Prayer, but the
process implied by "forgive us" differs from that expressed as
"as we forgive."

Forgiving others is therapeutic forgiveness: self-directed,
aimed at healing the self of emotional pain, conflict, or crisis.
When we experience this type of forgiveness, there is an emotional
release or catharsis that simultaneously calms and resolves the
underlying issues. Often the offender may not be, and does not
need to be, involved in this process. We forgive. The desired
outcome of forgiving others (including ourselves as "others") is
self-healing—purifying the self by purging it of anger, unresolved
conflicts, and frustrations. Counseling, whether faith-based or
not, desires to help us heal and get over unforgiveness when we
have been severely offended by someone or have internalized
negative impressions or criminalized ourselves.

On the other hand, when we say, "Forgive us our trespasses,"
we are asking God to forgive our sins against Him. Because the
scriptures affirm that God by His very nature is compassionate
and gracious, there is the assumption that His forgiveness is

guaranteed. Jonah, after surviving a suicide attempt in his bid to avoid going on an errand to Nineveh, came to this conclusion: "I knew that you are a gracious and compassionate God, slow to anger, abounding in faithful love, and one who relents from sending disaster" (Jonah 4:2b CSB).

The Psalmist expanded on this quality of God:

> He forgives all your iniquity; he heals all your diseases.
> He redeems your life from the Pit; he crowns you with faithful love and compassion.
> He satisfies you with good things; your youth is renewed like the eagle.
> The Lord executes acts of righteousness and justice for all the oppressed.
> He revealed his ways to Moses, his deeds to the people of Israel.
> The Lord is compassionate and gracious, slow to anger and abounding in faithful love.
> He will not always accuse us or be angry forever.
> He has not dealt with us as our sins deserve or repaid us according to our iniquities.
> For as high as the heavens are above the earth, so great is his faithful love toward those who fear him.
> As far as the east is from the west, so far has he removed our transgressions from us.
> As a father has compassion on his children, so the Lord has compassion on those who fear him.
> For he knows what we are made of, remembering that we are dust. (Psalm 103:3–14 CSB)

In Psalm 86:15 (CSB), similar sentiments are expressed: "But you, Lord, are a compassionate and gracious God, slow to anger and abounding in faithful love and truth."

Moreover, Jesus was crucified as atonement for our sins, as Paul testifies in Hebrews 2:17 (CSB):

> Therefore, he had to be like his brothers and sisters in every way, so that he could become a merciful and faithful high priest in matters pertaining to God, to make atonement for the sins of the people.

All that is true. God is ready and willing to forgive our sins and reconcile with us. He sent His only begotten son to die in atonement for our sins. Yet there is a condition for accessing this free and available pardon from sin: repentance. The forgiveness of our sins reconciles us with Holy God—God by His nature is willing and ready to forgive us our trespasses against Him, for which Jesus paid the full blood price. Yet repentance is a bridge to gaining His forgiveness.

Forgiving those who offend us is therapeutic and self-healing, while God's forgiveness of our trespasses against Him requires a secondary factor. As you may be quick to infer from the Lord's Prayer, forgiving those who trespass against us alone without repenting from the evil we have committed against God does not guarantee God's forgiveness. We must recognize a relevant differentiating factor between the forgiveness that heals our emotions and resolves psychological pathology on the one hand, and the forgiveness that on the other hand reconciles, predicated on expressing sincere remorse, guilt feelings, or repentance. The forgiveness that reconciles requires an acknowledging offender who is remorseful and repentant.

Forgiveness is stratified. If you desire God's forgiveness, have you repented of your wrongdoing? This verse of the Lord's Prayer seems to suggest that the more we are willing and able to forgive those who have offended us, the greater the likelihood God will forgive our sins—but not without repentance of our own sins or offenses against God.

Repentance-induced forgiveness furthers reconciliation. The catalytic effect of repentance requires a minimum of two parties to produce reconciliation. In this form of forgiveness, the offender and the offended might share blame and guilt for the offensive situation in whatever proportion. Of importance is that one or all parties take responsibility and are ready to be fully accountable for the transgression, to express sincere remorse, to regret what happened, and to commit to not repeating the incidence. When parties to a painful conflict share blame and guilt for a situation, reconciliation is the goal; the proportion of apportioning blame and guilt becomes irrelevant. When a party is willing to accept full responsibility for inflicting injury and pain on another, then reconciliation calls for forgiveness through repentance that is voluntary.

The Good News for the followers of Christ calls for repentance that we may be reconciled with the Holy God. We are wholly and fully responsible for our sins as individuals, communities, and countries. If the salvation of our souls with ultimate reconciliation with God is our desire, then belief in the Son of God is a mandatory condition. The Gospel of John gospel declares:

> Just as Moses lifted up the snake in the wilderness, so the son of Man must be lifted up, so that everyone who believes in Him may have eternal life. For God loved the world in this way: He gave His one and only Son, so that everyone who believes in Him will not perish but have eternal life. (John 3:14–16 CSB)

> The one who believes in the Son has eternal life, but the one who rejects the Son will not see life: instead, the wrath of God remains on him. (John 3:36 CSB)

There is a second condition that is equally mandatory for the salvation of souls and our ultimate reconciliation with God: forgiveness of our sins through repentance. This requirement for salvation is underscored by the first word recorded in the Gospel of Matthew to be spoken by Jesus Christ: "Repent" (Matthew 4:17).

Christ's harbinger is recorded in Mark 1:4: "John came baptizing in the wilderness and proclaiming a baptism of **repentance for the forgiveness of sin**" (Mark 1:4 CSB; emphasis mine), for the time has come to "repent and believe the good news" (Mark1:15(CSB). Yes! Repent and believe. The two pillars of salvation.

Having started His ministry with the word "repent," Jesus, at His farewell party just before His ascension, reminded the disciples of their mission:

> He also said to them, "This is what is written: The Messiah would suffer and rise from the dead the third day, and **repentance for forgiveness of sins** would be proclaimed in His name to all nations beginning at Jerusalem. (Luke 24: 46–47 CSB; emphasis mine)

Mark's gospel records this in the passage known as the Great Commission:

> Then He said to them, "Go into all the world and preach the gospel to all creation. Whosoever believes and is baptized will be saved, but whosoever does not believe will be condemned. (Mark 16:13–16 CSB)

The core directive of the commission is to be baptized to repentance for the forgiveness of sins. The signs listed thereafter are not part of the assignment. There is no place in the four Gospels where the performance of miracles, speaking in tongues, driving out demons, or and picking up snakes is an indication of salvation. Rather, Jesus said,

> "Not everyone who says to me, 'Lord, Lord,' will enter the kingdom of heaven, but only the one who does the will of my Father in heaven. On that day many will say to me, 'Lord, Lord, didn't we prophesy in your name, drive out demons in your name, and do many miracles in your name?'" (Matthew 7:21–22 CSB)

There was once a viral video about someone who calls himself a man of God and sits on a golden chair, beating his chest and yelling, "No one can take my church from me, the church I built with my money." He brags about how he would fast for a thousand days, and his God will rain vengeance on anyone who dares to interfere in his church. Apostle P. A. A. Egabor, General Evangelist of Christ Apostolic Church, always had this reminder: "True success is ending up in heaven."

Matthew tells us to "enter through the narrow gate. For the gate is wide and the road broad that leads to destruction, and there are many who go through it. (But) narrow is the gate and difficult the road that leads to life" (Matthew 7:13–14 CSB). The two sides of this narrow gate are believing in the Son of God and repentance. Both conditions are mandatory. It is not either/or, but both. Salvation is personal and comes only to those who believe and seek forgiveness by confessing and repenting of their sins.

Repentance is of such importance that there can be no salvation without it. We all sin and continue daily to offend God by omission or commission. No one should expect reconciliation with God without His pardon and forgiveness. In our relationship with God, we are completely responsible for our transgressions against Him. There are no greater sins or lesser sins leading to greater sinners or lesser sinners, "for all have sinned and fall short of the glory of God" (Romans 3:23 CSB).

Even on occasion, as when Jesus was tempted to condemn Pilate for his violent disposition, Jesus responded with a warning about the need for repentance. Jesus was informed that Pilate had used the blood of some Galileans as part of a sacrifice. Instead of speaking to the dastardly nature of this act, Jesus responded on the need for repentance. He pointed out that not experiencing disaster in our lives is not evidence that we are lesser sinners. His response is recorded thus in the Gospel of Luke:

> And he responded to them, "Do you think that these Galileans were more sinful than all the other Galileans because they suffered these things? No, I tell you; **but unless you repent**, you will all perish as well. Or those eighteen that the tower in Siloam fell on and killed—do you think they were more sinful than all the other people who live in Jerusalem? No, I tell you; **but unless you repent,** you will all perish as well." (Luke 13:2–5 CSB; emphasis mine)

The miracles happened. He raised the dead, opened blind eyes, healed the lame, empathized with the bereaved, and fed the hungry. But the recurring theme of Jesus's message is repentance. There is a universality to the need for repentance in our relationship with God.

> If we say, "We have no sin," we are deceiving ourselves, and the truth is not in us. If we confess our sins, he is faithful and righteous to forgive us our sins and to cleanse us from all unrighteousness.

If we say, "We have not sinned," we make him a liar and his word is not in us. (1 John 1:8–10 CSB)

If we confess our sins and repent, God is faithful to His word to forgive and reconcile with us. According to Richard Owens Roberts,

> To assume that sinners can turn to the Righteous One without turning from their own unrighteousness is the height of theological nonsense...There is no question as to the thrust of Christ's words: repentance is not merely a necessity for high-profile sinners. Every person is a sinner and every sinner must repent. Repentance is as mandatory for kings and presidents and rulers in every realm as it is for the common sinners. Popes, bishops, archbishops, priests, ministers, elders, deacons, and all in the ecclesiastical superstructure need to repent as greatly as do all the lay folk. Repentance is as needful for children as for fathers and mothers. The hardened criminal is no more in need of repentance than any other sinner of any sort. There is something very hypocritical about concluding that the subjects of calamity are greater sinners and therefore in more need of repentance than those who have long enjoyed peace and prosperity.[11]

"Forgive us our trespasses" requires that we repent. This is theme of the Gospels, for Christ came to call sinners to repentance: "I have not come to call the righteous, but sinners to repentance" (Luke 5:32 CSB). This verse excludes all self-righteous believers

---

[11] Richard Owen Roberts, *Repentance: The First Word of the Gospel* (Wheaton, IL: Crossway, 2002), pp. 17, 66.

from salvations. They are believers but think they have no need for forgiveness through repentance.

> When Jesus heard this, he told them, "It is not those who are well who need a doctor, but those who are sick. I did not come to call the righteous, but sinners." (Mark 2:17 CSB)

The parable of the lost son, also known as the prodigal son (Luke 15:11–31), presents two brothers on the two sides of repentance: an elder brother who is self-righteous and feels no need for repentance, and the younger brother who acknowledges his sins, repents, and seeks forgiveness. The younger brother's sins are vividly described—he took his share of their father's wealth and left home to squander his portion. He confesses to his wayward behavior and feels unworthy. His return home is cause for his father's celebration. On the flip side is his big brother, who stayed at home and worked hard on increasing the father's estate, never disobeying his father's orders. The sins of the elder brother are not so overtly enumerated because he stayed home and continued to be productive in the vineyard. But his anger, jealousy, and pride surfaced when he heard of the party for his brother.

Consistent with His pattern of packaging each parable or teaching with multiple lessons, Jesus used these brothers to teach on two different character traits relative to repentance. The character of the stay-at-home elder brother highlights the fact that while we may yet be deployed in the vineyard, we always have need for repentance. Our sins may not be obvious. Are we leaders of megachurches, speaking in tongues and yet unable to speak truth to political leadership, like the prophet Nathan? Our sins are not obvious. Do we look the other way while those who do not look like us are killed on the streets by law enforcement? Our sins are not obvious. Are we complicit in denying immigrants, those escaping hunger and suffering, from entering our homes, our states, and our country? Our sins are not so obvious. We preach fear and hatred from the pulpit and endorse political leadership bereft of any of the Fruits of the Spirit. Our sins are not so obvious. We speak lies from the pulpit and endorse lying tongues. Our sins are not so obvious. The privilege of serving in the Father's vineyard is extension of His Grace that covers our sins.

The elder son who stayed at home will not join and partake of a celebration. Why? The party was called for the younger brother, who had taken his share of their father's estate and squandered it abroad. Big brother did not forgive his younger brother and "became angry and didn't want to go in" (Luke 15:28 CSB) to the party to celebrate the return of the squanderer. We may not know the heart of God; I will not claim to know the heart of God, but the Bible makes it clear that anger borne out of unforgiveness for a brother, or a sister restrains us from God's blessings or from his party for us: "But I tell you, everyone who is angry with his brother or sister will be subject to judgment" (Matthew 5:22a CSB).

If the repentance and return of the overtly sinful prodigal son is cause for celebration, how much more rejoicing will there be if the elder brother repents?

In Matthew 21:28–32, Jesus used another parable of two sons to underscore the theme of his message: change of mind. The first son was sent to work on the vineyard. This son talked back to his father. In some cultures, that by itself is sacrilege. He did not hide his rebellious attitude and disobedience. This son told his father he was not going on the errand but later changed his mind and went. The second son offered "eye-service" to his father. He told the father he was going to work in the vineyard when in fact he had no intention of going and never did. Jesus came to point to this need for changing direction from disobedience and rebellion to salvation. Jesus asked,

> "Which of the two did his father's will?" They
> said, "The first." Jesus said to them, "Truly I tell

you, tax collectors and prostitutes are entering the
kingdom of God before you. For John came to
you in the way of righteousness, and you didn't
believe him. Tax collectors and prostitutes did
believe him; but you, when you saw it, didn't
even change your minds then and believe him."
(Matthew 21:28–32 CSB)

Salvation is for those who believe, repent, and return from their
evil ways. Our gift of prophesy, speaking in tongues, or performing
miracles does not confer salvation. When Jesus referenced the
miracles He performed, it was for the purpose of underscoring
the need for repentance. Miracles help to reaffirm the existence
of the supernatural, the God of the impossible. However, beyond
the excitement and joy of being the recipient of a miracle is the
call to repentance. Jesus comments on the connection of His
miracles to repentance:

> Then he proceeded to denounce the towns where
> most of his miracles were done, because they did
> not repent: "Woe to you, Chorazin! Woe to you,
> Bethsaida! For **if the miracles that were done
> in you had been done in Tyre and Sidon, they
> would have repented** in sackcloth and ashes long
> ago. (Matthew 11:20–21 CSB; emphasis mine)

We are thankful for God's everyday miracles, which point to
His existence and continued influence in and on the universe.
However, we get stuck on the miracles, rejoice, celebrate, and
forget to decipher the meaning or purpose of the miracles. The
miracles we experience must transform us and change us from
the inside, drawing us to the greatest miracle of all: repentance.
Miracles performed in the name of Jesus Christ are meant to draw
us to repentance.

CHAPTER 5

WHAT IS SIN? WHEN DO WE NEED FORGIVENESS?

When do we know we have sinned against God and are in need of repentance? This is the question that confronts us when seeking to establish issues that call for the need for forgiveness. Is sin against God defined by the culturally acceptable or normative behavior of our community or society? It is open knowledge that man has perpetrated evil and wickedness on follow human beings since time immemorial. What about the politician who diverts public funds into his personal bank account outside his country while the people of his country suffer in poverty, ignorance, and disease? Does he perceive evil and sin in his actions? After all, the people he so deprives of amenities sing his praises and bestow titles on him. If the culture accepts divorce, is the man who has multiple marriages, each ending in divorce, sinful? Or is it sinful for a man to legally have more than one consenting wife? Should our culture define when we seek God's forgiveness? Whose culture?

Are we evil and sinful if the wickedness in us is conceived only in our thoughts and imagination but not expressed as actions? This lack of universality in defining what is evil in our minds and to our eyes becomes problematic when we seek to present a universal concept of what is evil and sinful, deserving of repentance and forgiveness from God.

In an article for *Psychiatric Annals*, Dr. Saul Levine acknowledged the problem of defining evil: "The truth is that a definition that is universally accepted is difficult to achieve. We can all conceptualize acts or conjure up images that might be perceived as evil by some. However, these same behaviors may be seen as understandable, legitimate, or even inspiring by others."[12] He goes on to tabulate nine perspectives from which evil can be defined.

THE CONCEPTS OF EVIL FROM DIFFERENT PERSPECTIVES
(from S. Levine, "The Development of Wickedness")

Discipline	Discourse	Dilemmas
Evolution	Evil is driven by the evolution of the species throughout the militia, a phylogenetically programmed phenomenon that has evolved because the very survival of the species depends on the "beastliness of man" (Plato, Hobbes, Nietzsche), According to natural selection (Darwin), evil has proven to be adaptive. Benevolent acts are only performed because of a "payoff" (reciprocal altruism)	In this scenario, there is no answer to the "evolutionary imperative" of evil. Little or nothing can be done to overcome Darwinian forces, which are developed and if anything, reinforced, through the millennia
Genetic	Evil is largely biologically driven, insofar as we are "prisoners" of our inherited genetic and chromosomal predispositions to misbehave. In this view, evil is instinctual, some of us are constitutionally programmed (see Demonic Man) to malignity.	If this perspective is valid, then perhaps a gene site, or cell substrate, can be manipulated. Perhaps "genetic engineering" or reprogramming" the double helix can be accomplished. Perhaps we can "screen" for gene types or aberrant gene sites.

---

[12] Saul Levine, "The Development of Wickedness—From Whence Does Evil Stem?" *Psychiatric Annals* 27:9 (September 1997), pp. 617–623.

Learning	Evil is learned from others in our midst (parents, media, peers, and others). It is externally and contextually driven. Evil is taught to us by modeling, mentoring, "osmosis." Reinforcement, imprinting, reward, and so on. From this perspective, as an integral part of our development, we incorporate the lessons of moral laxity and malevolent manipulation of others for nefarious gains, and in so doing, become deviant ourselves.	We would have to "deprogram" and reteach the captive evil mind. However, we can prevent the appearance of evil by proper teaching and reinforcement of benevolent behavior. The social context can be changed, rewards and punishments can be redirected in a strategic "protocol", using learning theory and behavioral techniques to shape the minds of our children according to this model, or reteach those who have learned "wrong" (ie, evil) behavior.
Pathological (Psychiatric)	The medical model holds that perpetrators of evil are sick; psychiatrically dysfunctional, disordered, and disturbed individuals, or that they have an abnormal characterologic disorder that accounts for their diseased minds and destructive behavior. This might be based on a neurotransmitter problem, or as a result of early trauma (eg, abuse), but the common end result is the "illness" of evil. Serial killers or the antisocial personality would be cases in point.	The sick obviously have to be diagnosed, treated, and cured. Evil should be analyzed scientifically and studied epidemiologically, so that incidence and prevalence can be ascertained. Eradication is then the attainable goal. This model also implies a preventive aspect; just as immunization eradicates certain diseases, so, too, desensitization or humanization (Salk) will prevent the "disease." Perhaps a "vaccine" can even be developed to this end. Certainly, we should be able to develop interventions (surgery, medications) to control the behavior of deviant individuals or even "cure" them.

Chemical	This purview is actually a subgroup of the pathological perspective. The evil behavior is attributable to external chemical agents, either inadvertently introduced or deliberately taken in order to change one's mood or perception. In this scenario, street drugs (eg, speed, cocaine, and others), potent allergens, toxins, and pollutants are included.	Obviously, the offending agent(s) must be removed from our midst – from circulation, availability, and air, water, and food supplies. Eradication of drugs and toxins has not proven to be extraordinarily successful.
Teleological	As in "the end justifies the means," in this scenario, acts of a repugnant, destructive nature are seen by the perpetrators and their supporters as rational and justified. Even malignant mayhem and cruel brutality, in this view, can be deemed as "acceptable," eg, "your" terrorist might well be "my" freedom fighter or revolutionary. Revenge ("getting even") or avenging the cruelty inflicted on you or yours serves as a "time-honored" rationale for malicious retribution. A particularly perverse "subform" of this perspective would deem abhorrent acts as acceptable if they serve a personal empowering or even creative personal function. This is the bizarre obverse of "growing through adversity," instead, it is "growing through hurting others!"	The problem with this perspective is that individual beliefs and perceptions largely determine the definition of evil. Obviously, if the act is in the very service of a cause you believe in passionately, you might be less inclined to ascribe malevolence to the perpetrators. You might even wish to honor them.

Moral-Theological	Evil is an expression of "original sin," of humankind's innate badness, our "natural" propensity to wickedness. In this view, our proclivities to sinning are part and parcel of our human and spiritual imperfections. Dybbuks and demons are Satan's way of testing and tormenting our spiritual authenticity. In the Judeo-Christian model, the parables of Adam and Eve, and especially Cain and Abel in the Old Testament and St Mark's teachings in the New Testament, serve as the analogy for man's sinning and God's punishment. Derived from this is punishment meted out by God to subsequent generations for continued or remorseless transgressions. Similarly, other holy books or tomes refer to our proclivities to sin and to the service of God as our only salvation.	Evil can only be exorcised by redemption of our soul, by giving one's self over to the Supreme Being, by genuinely atoning, by asking for forgiveness, by upholding the highest standards of moral and ethical behavior (ie, that which is contained in the Ten Commandments and other Deity-inspired laws). Because humankind inherently "knows" what is good and what is evil, forgiveness is only contingent on repentance.
Criminological-Correctional	This view holds that evil is only the domain of bad people who do bad things, that most people are pristine in thought and behavior, and that our world would be a better place if only those rotten apples were removed from our inherently bountiful barrel of goodness. Causes/considerations and etiology are not important; bad behavior is only concern	The "whys' and "wherefores" are totally irrelevant; evildoers must be apprehended, disciplined, punished, removed from the rest of us blessed souls of virtue, and not released unless and until we have "proof" of total rehabilitation, remorse, or sufficient exacting of retributive "justice."

| Political-
Socioeconomic
Cultural | Obviously, parts of these disciplines are subsumed under the teleological and learning perspectives, as in, we learn what we are taught, and then can rationalize our malevolent behavior. Who has not fought a battle without a feeling of self-righteousness and moral justification, and that "God is on our side" (Bob Dylan)? If the Serbs are right, what about Croats and Muslims? If the Protestants in Dublin are right, what about the Catholics? If the Tutsis are justified, what about the Hutus? If the Jihad is justified, what about the Israelis' perception? And so it goes ... (Kurt Vonnegut Jr.) | Pacts, treaties, demilitarization, tribunals, United Nations, World Court, free trade, the teachings of the Bible (or Koran, and others), education, and so on, all com to mind as examples of attempts to eradicate hostility, hate and Holocaust. Thus far, Homo Sapiens has failed miserably in their endeavors. |

Distinguishing "good" from "bad" or "evil" actions and behavior is problematic to the extent that there seems to be no unanimity in what is morally right or wrong. In *Philosophy of Religion*, C. Stephen Evans discussed arguments against accepting the proposition that "there are objectively binding moral obligations." These arguments include the concept of *"cultural relativism* which interprets moral obligations in terms of social approval and disapproval. Every society approves and disapproves of actions and expresses their approval and disapproval by training the young to think of those actions as 'right' or 'wrong.' Which acts are designated as right or wrong differ from culture to culture."[13] A universal standard of morals becomes difficult to define, as no one culture can be adjudged superior or inferior to another. An extreme version of cultural relativism is "individual relativism"—

---

[13] C. Stephen Evans, *Philosophy of Religion: Thinking about Faith* (Downers Grove, IL: IVP Academics, 1985). p 70.

whatever the individual considers as right and good is right and good for him or her. And a further modification of this concept says, "when a person says that an act is wrong, she is not stating a fact but only expressing her individual emotions or attitudes about the act."[14] This is *ethical emotivism*—if you maliciously slap me and leave me with a black eye, that such blatant violation gives you pleasure does not make the action right. It is funny because you the perpetrator finds it funny and right. My feeling that I have been wronged should matter.

If we step back and recognize and accept the oneness of humans and define humanity as one, then universally binding moral standards will become obvious—the binding moral obligations that will be universal and common to a single global human community and culture and not cultures established through an "us" versus "them" configuration. It will become obvious that a Creator responsible for putting us all here has guiding principles for how we relate with one another. Much of our moral obligation to one another is a matter of respecting the worth and value of the person irrespective of which continent we find ourselves, or of our color, creed, religion, language, or nationality. A universal morality must be grounded on the rules of love and respect for one another established by the Creator—God, the Supreme Being. Evans puts it this way: "God is the Supreme Reality, and He is supremely good and loving; we therefore have an obligation to love and respect Him, as well as His creatures, especially those creatures made in His image." This is the source of an objectively binding moral obligation, the point that defines the unity of humankind.

Any definition of evil that establishes an "us" versus "them" upfront perceives evil from the victor's perspective. In a binary arrangement, the defeated, powerless, and subjugated will be presented as evil when humanity is polarized. The underdog

---

[14] Evans, p. 71.

who loses becomes the sinner in a bipolar world. The winners get to define what is good, as they define the dominant culture and acceptable norm. The goodness that is defined in the terms of the strong, the winner, is then deployed in the service of the culture subsequently established. The subdued is evil, "savage," and outcast if they hold on to their position; the circumstances producing their belief and behavior are given no consideration and do not need to be explored and understood. Our ethnocentric tendencies perpetuate a nose-in-the-air attitude of "my culture is superior to your culture." In the event of a culture war, the community that loses is inferior and evil. What is weak is often not given due respect and does not contribute to defining what is evil. We human beings do not have any locus from which we can categorize others as evil or sinners, for humanity is one and there is only one human race. "Good" and "bad" on our terms sets humanity into two groups, "us" and "them."

Friedrich Nietzsche for instance categorized two types of morality in <u>*On the Genealogy of Morals*</u>. He wrote:

> Now it is plane to me, first of all, that in this theory the source of the concept "good" has been sought and established in the wrong place: the judgment "good" did not originate with those to whom "goodness" was shown! Rather it was "the good" themselves, that is to say, the noble, powerful, high-stationed, and high-minded, who felt and established themselves and their actions as good, that is, of the first rank, in contradistinction to all the low, low-minded, common and plebeian.[15]

---

[15] Friedrich Nietzsche, *On The Genealogy of Morals*, (New York: Vintage, 1967), p. 25.

He posited that these self-anointed "good" people define a noble or master morality and rate behaviors as either good or bad. By their standard, the morality of nobility and the strong-willed accords honor and creates values for things. In master morality, the individuals who "designate themselves simply by their superiority in power"[16] define what is good based on whether it benefits them and the pursuit of their self-defined personal excellence. The strong-willed define as good only those values that help them attain lifelong self-actualization. Nietzsche called the opposite of master morality "slave morality," a reactionary morality aimed at devaluing the values of the strong-willed.

> The slave revolt in morality begins when *ressentiment* itself becomes creative and gives birth to values: the ressentiment of natures that are denied the true reaction, that of deeds, and compensate themselves with an imaginary revenge. While every noble morality develops from a triumphant affirmation of itself, slave morality from the outset says No to what is "outside", what is "different", what is "not itself"; and this No is its creative deed. ...In order to exist, slave morality always first needs a hostile external world ...its action is fundamentally reaction.[17]

This inverse of the master and noble morality is characterized by pessimism and cynicism. This polarization of morality, even within a homogenous community, denies the unity and oneness of the community. The strong and powerful define what is good, and the loser is evil and bad. Only the deprived, disadvantaged underdog can commit evil deeds.

---

[16] Nietzsche, p. .
[17] Nietzsche, pp. 36–37.

The Creator of humanity, before whom the human race is one family, is the source of a universal definition of what is good or bad. Evil occurs when any part of humanity is maliciously and unjustly hurt. There is evil when we look the other way as those who do not look like us are subject to extrajudiciary execution on the streets. There is evil when we turn our backs on the poor and hungry among us. There is evil when we breed *talakawas* in Nigeria and feed them lies about religion and ethnicity. There is evil when people run to us from suffering, and we deny them entry or take them as slaves. There is evil when we acclaim lying leaders from the pulpit or we are unable to speak truth to leadership. There is evil when our truth is colored by race, religion, ethnicity, and language. The evil among us goes beyond sexual immorality, abortion, petty stealing, and such individualized transgressions.

The scriptures present a solution to the lack of unanimity in conceiving of what to consider evil and sinful. All of humanity does evil against God, the Supreme Being who is Creator and owner of all. To echo King David, against God and God alone do we sin. He does not discriminate for or against persons, beliefs, or cultures. There is no "us" or "them" with Him. He allows the sun to rise and set over all. He allows rain to fall equally for the benefit of all. This central and common factor provides a universal basis for conceiving what is good and what is bad in our values and actions.

The origin of humanity's sinfulness is clearly recorded in the narration of Genesis, chapter 3. Our morality does not define what is sin and evil before God. Our morality may establish codes of what we perceive as respectful, ethical, and acceptable ways of relating with one another. Hence these standards vary from family to family, from community to community, and from nation to nation. However, the story in Genesis defines sin and evil from a central perceptive that evil is humanity's disobedience to God's orders. This is the common factor that provides for a universality to the concept of sin and what is evil.

The biblical story of creation is all so familiar that repeating it would be redundant. The narration establishes God's characteristic nature of grace. Adam and Eve experienced God's grace with a purpose declared in Genesis 1:28. God pronounced a blessing over them. They were to be productive and increase, subdue and fill the earth, rule, and control all other living things. There was no limitation, as they were conferred with full and absolute authority over all of creation—God's unlimited unconditional love.

> God blessed them, and God said to them, "Be fruitful, multiply, fill the earth, and subdue it. Rule the fish of the sea, the birds of the sky, and every creature that crawls on the earth." (Genesis 1:28 CSB)

In Genesis 2:16–17, there was an addendum, and this is where the first "don't" is introduced. Every plant that God made they could eat of, with one exemption. This exemption was conspicuously located in the center of the garden. It was unique and different.

> And the Lord God commanded the man, "You are free to eat from any tree of the garden, but you **must not** eat from the tree of the knowledge of good and evil, for on the day you eat from it, you will certainly die." (Genesis 2:16–17 CSB)

We are not given the duration of time Adam and Eve complied with not eating from the forbidden tree. But eventually they failed. They disobeyed. This act of disobedience of their Creator's clear instructions is the fundamental principle that underlies sin. Eve was reminded of God's instructions, and Genesis 2:2–3 shows that she recalled the totality of the orders and possible consequences. The violation under this setting is not due to tricky manipulation, temptation, or a weakness such as poor memory or human defect, as is often attributed to the act. As happens today, we flagrantly disobey God in the pretense that "God is doing a new thing." We violate His orders on our self-proclaimed exemption from the rules. We reframe and rationalize our sinful acts in terms of our dominant culture.

Before taking of the apple and eating the fruit of the tree in the middle of the garden, Eve and her husband reviewed the rules and the prescribed consequences but decided to disobey. They choose to be independent from God's instruction. Adam and Eve had authority and dominion over the tempter identified as Serpent. They named it along with naming all other God's creations. The compelling thinking that persuaded them to disobey their Creator on the mere advice of a subordinate being seem unconvincing.

> Now the serpent was the most cunning of all the wild animals that the Lord God had made. He said to the woman, "Did God really say, 'You can't eat from any tree in the garden'?" The woman said to the serpent, "We may eat the fruit from the trees in the garden. But about the fruit of the tree in the middle of the garden, God said, 'You must not eat it or touch it, or you will die.'" "No! You will certainly not die," the serpent said to the woman. "In fact, God knows that when you eat it your eyes will be opened and you will be like God, knowing good and evil." The woman saw that the tree was good for food and delightful to look at, and that it was desirable for obtaining wisdom. So she took some of its fruit and ate it; she also gave some to her husband, who was with her, and he ate it. Then the eyes of both of them were opened, and they knew they were naked; so,

> they sewed fig leaves together and made coverings
> for themselves. (Genesis 3:1–7 CSB)

Adam and his wife resorted to blame-shifting when they were confronted on their act of disobedience. Adam was unable to take responsibility for his actions, and neither was Eve. Adam's defense was more like, "I have been here tending your garden faithfully and obediently until you gave me a wife that I did not request. See the harm you caused." Adam blamed God for Adam's disobedience. Today, we multiply this reasoning. God's benevolence, His beneficence and love, and His grace is why we disobey Him. The injustice and pervasive suffering humankind inflicts on itself is blamed on God's supremacy. We are unable to take responsibility for our failures. Theodicy quickly comes to the rescue.

How come there is so much evil and sin in the presence of an all-knowing, all-powerful, and benevolent God? Human beings are unwilling to accept responsibility for the evil they perpetuate. They define alternative rules embedded in cultural morality established by the conqueror for the conquered among us. We define alternatives where God has created absolutes. Male and female He made us. Humanity blames the Creator and creates a spectrum in this bipolar establishment. It must be confusing. We cannot seem to figure out that "male and female" has no in-between.

Besides blaming God for our sinful nature today, we double back and blame Adam and Eve. If they had not disobeyed, there would be no "original sin," and we would not have our present-day sinful nature. We would not sin if Adam and Eve had not sinned. Good for them. After all, they started the blame game.

The so-called original sin is not why we disobey God today. God does not seem to be interested in our rationalization of why we violate Him. His mercy and grace call us to be accountable and responsible for our violations. He calls us to repentance and not rationalization. He calls us to return to Him. This is the meeting point for our diverse cultures, nationalities, moralities, race, color, and language when considering the universality of what needs to be considered as sin. God defines it. To write in English, the Creator is identified as God. Your indigenous or ethnic language might dictate differently. The exaggerated apportioning of blame to the sin of Adam and Eve (original sin) for our sinful nature today safely avoids owning our faults and disobedience towards God. We ignore the truth that every individual is responsible for his own sin and that the doctrine (dogma) of "inherited" or "biologically transmitted" sin is inherently faulty. Even our man-made judicial system will not be equitable if the child is adjudged guilty by virtue of the ancestor's offense.

> The Prophet Ezekiel declared from the Lord God, What do you mean by using this proverb concerning the land of Israel: "The fathers eat sour grapes, and the children's teeth are set on edge"? As I live—this is the declaration of the Lord God—you will no longer use this proverb in Israel. Look, every life belongs to me. The life of the father is like the life of the son—both belong to me. The person who sins is the one who will die. (Ezekiel 18:2–4 CSB)

This declaration does not sound ambiguous: the person who sins is the one who gets punished. Ezekiel narrated scenarios of a righteous parent who faithfully obeys God's statute but has a violent child who is fraudulent and does not follow after his father's righteousness. Will the child not be punished for his transgressions? And suppose another child whose parent was sinful does not offend after the manner of the parent—will that child be punished like the parent who sinned? While the offending parent and the offending child will deserve their punishment, the non-offending child of an offending parent does not deserve punishment. Adam and Eve's disobedience of God does not confer punishment on us.

> But you may ask, "Why doesn't the son suffer
> punishment for the father's iniquity?" Since the son
> has done what is just and right, carefully observing
> all my statutes, he will certainly live. The person
> who sins is the one who will die. A son won't suffer
> punishment for the father's iniquity, and a father
> won't suffer punishment for the son's iniquity. The
> righteousness of the righteous person will be on
> him, and the wickedness of the wicked person will
> be on him. (Ezekiel 18:19–20 CSB)

The narrative of Genesis 3 provides an insight into how we might offend God and be out of His favor and grace. It does not confer sin on us nor make us predisposed to sin. It establishes a universal principle that defines how we might offend God through disobedience, defiantly pursuing our own independence from His will, and seeking to attain our own moral autonomy. Sin is our unwillingness to be compliant with the Creator's orders, our desire to be our own creator, the source of our own existence. We sin when we seek to self-validate our actions and behavior or elevate others, including things, to the position of validating our actions and behaviors. This search for self-justification and recognition of our actions from others requires that fellow human beings do for us what only God could do for us. This is idolatry! "Whoever (or whatever) is harnessed into an event of self-justification is also made into an idol in the process."[18]

In Genesis, chapter 4, the need for man to self-validate his actions is presented to underline our defiance when sinning

---

[18] Christof Gestrich, *The Return of Splendor into the World The Christian Doctrine of Sin and Forgiveness*, (Grand Rapids, MI/Cambridge, England, 1997), p. 176.

against God. Cain presented an offering to God that was not satisfactory. (I guess he is not alone in not liking an F for a grade!) Cain is frustrated and angry because his offering was not accepted by God. Cain becomes so distraught and depressed that he nurses homicidal thoughts towards his brother, Abel. In the story, between the presentation of offering that is rejected and Cain murdering his brother, there is verse 7 (see passage following). God had a discussion with Cain and gave him counsel with some advice. You do not need to be angry and sad; if your offering is right, it will be accepted. For now, sin is crouching, hanging out outside the door of your heart. Do not let it in. You must overcome thoughts of doing evil. As gruesome as the act of killing a brother is, Cain defiantly ignored God's intervention. Cain did not kill Abel because Adam and Eve, his parents, had been disobedient against God. Just as we continue to ignore God's counsel today, Cain ignored God and followed his own counsel. And after the act, he had a prepared query for God, "Am I my brother's keeper?"

> In the course of time Cain presented some of the land's produce as an offering to the Lord. And Abel also presented an offering—some of the firstborn of his flock and their fat portions. The Lord had regard for Abel and his offering, but he did not have regard for Cain and his offering. Cain was furious, and he looked despondent. Then the Lord said to Cain, "Why are you furious? And why do you look despondent? If you do what is right, won't you be accepted? But if you do not do what is right, sin is crouching at the door. Its desire is for you, but you must rule over it." Cain said to his brother Abel, "Let's go out to the field." And while they were in the field, Cain attacked his brother Abel and killed him. Then the Lord said to Cain, "Where is your brother Abel?" "I don't

know," he replied. "Am I my brother's guardian?" (Genesis 4:3–9 CSB)

Sin is wanting to be unaccountable to the Supreme Being, wanting to be self-sufficient in claiming to do for ourselves what only God can do for us. Humanity overestimates its capability and capacity without God, and in so doing it exposes itself to temptations that reveal its weaknesses. When so confronted, Man resorts to defying God's orders, out of forgetfulness or seeking to be independent; and undermining the respect of others. Christof Gestrich puts it this way:

> Sin is nothing specifically moral. Immorality is not the same as sin. Sin is a far-reaching category to which questions of morality are also related. The word "sin" describes our life from God's viewpoint. Our life does not hear "anything" from God. As sinners, we stand before the silent God…For man himself is the origin of evil. His exocentric position in the cosmos (his specific intellectual faculties) causes him to be tempted time and again to turn his own merely fleeting and relative significance deceitfully into absolute significance. In this way he disrupts the cosmos and destroys himself and others. In this way too, he sins and forfeits his relative freedom because he yields to temptation and deludes himself about his true condition.[19]

Morality that is relative to the values of our community fall short in defining what is sin against God. The standards and values of cultural morals to establish what is right or wrong are

---

[19] Gestrich, *The Return of Splendor*, pp. 79, 151.

limited to the community where they are defined. Within the community, such morality reflects a willingness collectively to defend what is acceptable and appropriate, just because of the community's shared humanity. Sharia law is a moral code in many Islamic communities, but it is not morally acceptable in non-Islamic communities; polygamy is morally acceptable in most indigenous African communities, and a High Priest of most African Traditional Religions is expected to have multiple wives, but this is not morally acceptable in many other communities of the world. Serial marriage accompanied by divorce is morally acceptable in Western communities but considered irresponsible in some societies. Societies that do not accept heterosexual polygamy may consider same sex marriage as a human right. What is evil and universally morally wrong can be defined only from God's perspective.

CHAPTER 6

THE PRINCIPLES OF REPENTANCE

C hrist's teachings and works, including miracles, were directed towards the main theme of His ministry: repentance and forgiveness. The Gospel of Luke, chapter fifteen, records three of His parables that emphasize the focus of His ministry for the audience: sinners. The first two parables, the parable of the lost sheep and that of the coin, feature items that were separated from the owner but lacked the ability to consciously contribute to reuniting with the master. The onus is on the owner to go find his lost sheep or coin, and when he finds them, he rejoices.

> So he told them this parable: "What man among you, who has a hundred sheep and loses one of them, does not leave the ninety-nine in the open field and go after the lost one until he finds it? When he has found it, he joyfully puts it on his shoulders, and coming home, he calls his friends and neighbors together, saying to them, 'Rejoice with me, because I have found my lost sheep!' I tell you, in the same way, there will be more joy in heaven over one sinner who repents than over ninety-nine righteous people who don't need repentance. Or what woman who has ten silver

coins, if she loses one coin, does not light a lamp, sweep the house, and search carefully until she finds it? When she finds it, she calls her friends and neighbors together, saying, 'Rejoice with me, because I have found the silver coin I lost!' I tell you, in the same way, there is joy in the presence of God's angels over one sinner who repents." (Luke 15:3–10 CSB)

However, the celebration in heaven on the return of a sinner is one half of what needs to consciously happen. The separation of the sheep and coin from their owners was physical and locational. However, it is sin that separates us from Holy God. We may yet be in the vineyard striving as hard as we can but separated from God by our not so obvious sins. We could be in His presence but separated by our sins.

Consider this story of the guy with his missing hat. A man once spent days looking for his hat. Finally, he decided that he would go to church on Sunday and sit at the back. During the service, he would sneak out and grab a hat from the rack at the front door. On Sunday, he went to church and sat at the back. The sermon was about the Ten Commandments. He sat through the whole sermon, and instead of sneaking out, he waited until the service was over and went to talk to the minister. "Father, I came here today to steal a hat to replace the one I lost. But after hearing your sermon on the Ten Commandments, I changed my mind."

The minister said, "Bless you, my son. Was it when I started to preach, 'Thou shall not steal' that changed your mind?"

The man replied, "No. It was the one on adultery. When you started to preach on that, I remembered where I left my hat."

We may be in the Lord's presence, even striving hard in the vineyard, yet powerfully separated from Him by our wrongdoings. This is a state of being present but absent.

Jesus followed the parables of the lost sheep and the lost coin with the parable of the lost son. One striking difference between the first two parables and the third parable is that the lost son was not found—the lost son *returned*. He returned repentant. Unlike the lost sheep and the lost coin, the prodigal son has a will and the ability to make choices. Jesus used the parable of the lost son to enumerate the necessary ingredients of repentance and reconciliation with the Father. Describing this son as "lost" relates the message of this parable to that of the parables of the lost sheep and the lost coin. The son was lost to his father because of both his offensive behavior and his physical separation from the father. Describing the son as "prodigal" identifies his character traits— reckless and wastefully extravagant, a spendthrift. If he returned home without addressing his prodigal nature, his return would not have been profitable. There would have been no rejoicing and celebration if he returned home without addressing the behavioral aspect of his separation.

The lost son's physical departure from home grieved his father. What grieved the father more was his premature claim to his inheritance and the squandering of it. Our geographical location does not separate us from God. Our sins separate us from our Father, God, who is ready to forgive us but waits for us to acknowledge that we have done wrong and to return to Him in repentance.

> After squandering his share of his father's estate, the prodigal son came to his senses. Then he said, "How many of my father's hired workers have more than enough food, and here I am dying of hunger! I'll get up, go to my father, and say to him, 'Father, I have sinned against heaven and in your sight. I am no longer worthy to be called your son. Make me like one of your hired workers.'" (Luke 15:17–19 CSB)

First, the sinner must recognize and acknowledge that they have erred against God as the prodigal son in the parable did. In the first book of Kings, King Solomon prayed that

> when they sin against you—for there is no one who does not sin—and you are angry with them and hand them to the enemy, and their captors deport them to the enemy's country—whether distant or nearby—and **when they come to their senses** in the land where they were deported **and repent and petition you** in their captors' land: **"We have sinned and done wrong; we have been wicked,"** and they return to you with their heart and all their soul in the land of their enemies who took them captive, and when they pray to you in the direction of their land that you gave their ancestors, the city you have chosen, and the temple I have built for your name, may you hear in heaven, your dwelling place, their prayer, and petition and uphold their cause. May you forgive your people who sinned against you and all their rebellion against you, and may you grant them compassion before their captors so that they may treat them compassionately. (1 Kings 8:46–50 CSB; emphasis mine)

Repentance requires that we can see and identify the specific nature of our errors, acknowledging the material particulars of errors rather than generalization—not "I stole from them" without stating the exact particulars of what was stolen and who "them" refers to. This would set the stage for meeting the second ingredient of repentance: confession, sincerely and freely stating our offense for which we seek forgiveness. Unlike Adam, who tried shifting the blame for his sin onto his wife, Eve, a truly penitent heart is self-incriminating and does not try to rationalize the offense. The prophet Daniel fasted, prayed, and confessed his sins and the sins of Israel to God without justifying their sins before God. Daniel recognized the specifics of their sins and prayed that God's wrath be turned away.

> Ah, Lord—the great and awe-inspiring God who keeps his gracious covenant with those who love him and keep his commands—**we have sinned, done wrong, acted wickedly, rebelled, and turned away from your commands and ordinances.** We have not listened to your servants the prophets, who spoke in your name to our kings, leaders, ancestors, and all the people of the land. Lord, righteousness belongs to you, but this day public shame belongs to us: the men of Judah, the residents of Jerusalem, and all Israel—those who are near and those who are far, in all the countries where you have banished them because of the disloyalty they have shown toward you. **Lord, public shame belongs to us, our kings, our leaders, and our ancestors, because we have sinned against you.** Compassion and forgiveness belong to the Lord our God, though we have rebelled against him and have not obeyed the Lord our God by following his instructions that he set before us through his servants the prophets. All Israel has broken your law and turned away, refusing to obey you. The promised curse written in the law of Moses, the servant of God, has been poured out on us because we have sinned against him. He has carried out his words that he spoke against us and against our rulers by bringing on us a disaster that is so great that nothing like what

has been done to Jerusalem has ever been done
under all of heaven. Just as it is written in the law
of Moses, all this disaster has come on us, yet we
have not sought the favor of the Lord our God by
turning from our iniquities and paying attention
to your truth. So the Lord kept the disaster in
mind and brought it on us, for the Lord our God
is righteous in all he has done. But we have not
obeyed him. Now, Lord our God—who brought
your people out of the land of Egypt with a strong
hand and made your name renowned as it is this
day—**we have sinned, we have acted wickedly.**
Lord, in keeping with all your righteous acts, may
your anger and wrath turn away from your city
Jerusalem, your holy mountain; for because of our
sins and the iniquities of our ancestors, Jerusalem
and your people have become an object of ridicule
to all those around us. Therefore, our God, hear
the prayer and the petitions of your servant. Make
your face shine on your desolate sanctuary for the
Lord's sake. Listen closely, my God, and hear. Open
your eyes and see our desolations and the city that
bears your name. For we are not presenting our
petitions before you based on our righteous acts,
but based on your abundant compassion. Lord,
hear! Lord, forgive! Lord, listen and act! My God,
for your own sake, do not delay, because your city
and your people bear your name. (Daniel 9:4–19
CSB; emphases mine)

True repentance must be self-indicting and remorseful.

Against you—you alone—I have sinned and done
this evil in your sight. So, you are right when you

pass sentence; you are blameless when you judge. (Psalm 51:4 CSB)

So I confess my iniquity; I am anxious because of my sin. (Psalm 38:18 CSB)

When we confess our sins, God's grace and mercy are magnified towards us.

When King David acknowledged his sins, the same prophet who confronted him with his sins delivered the pardon of God. In the same vein, when one of the thieves crucified with Christ confessed to his sins and acknowledge that he was justly punished, he obtained instant pardon and a reward of paradise.

David responded to Nathan, "I have sinned against the Lord." Then Nathan replied to David, "And the Lord has taken away your sin; you will not die." (2 Samuel 12:13 CSB)

"We are punished justly, because we're getting back what we deserve for the things we did, but this man has done nothing wrong." Then he said, "Jesus, remember me when you come into your kingdom." And he said to him, "Truly I tell you, today you will be with me in paradise." (Luke 23:41–43 CSB)

In his 1668 work *Doctrine of Repentance*, the English Puritan preacher and author Thomas Watson described the true penitent thus:

A true penitent confesses that he mingles sin with all that he does, and therefore has nothing to boast of. Uzziah, though a king, yet had a leprosy in his forehead; he had enough to abase him (2 Chron. 26:19). So a child of God, even when he does good, yet acknowledges much evil to be in that good. This lays all his feathers of pride in the dust.[20]

The truly penitent heart grieves the offense rather than the punishment. The prodigal son did not plead guilty but passed judgment on himself. He would rather be a servant than be called a son.

King David, at the apex of his reign, after killing his thousand and ten thousand in defense of Israel, took time off to commit adultery with the wife of his general Uriah. To cover his adultery, he set Uriah up to be killed (2 Samuel 11). In chapter 12, the story continues with the Lord sending the prophet Nathan to reprimand His Highness, King David. Nathan introduces his missive to the king with a parable that drew David's anger. The king was infuriated that a rich man who had "very large flocks and herbs" would take a poor man's only little ewe to feast his visitor. David was quick with his verdict: "As the Lord lives, the man who did this deserves to die!" (2 Samuel 12:5 CSB). When "the man who did this" turned out to be David himself, his verdict did not change: "David responded to Nathan, 'I have sinned against the Lord'" (2 Samuel 12:13 CSB). David owned up to his misbehavior and poor judgment; he was remorseful, sincerely repentant, and did not seek to rationalize or shift blame.

In Psalm 15, David espouses his concept of integrity. Who is it that dwells in the house of the Lord? One who is blameless, righteous, and acknowledges the truth in his heart, one who does not backbite, slander, and use his tongue to kill his neighbor, and one who "keeps his words no matter the cost" (verse 4b). When

[20] Thomas Watson, *Doctrine of Repentance*, (Cambridge, England/ Carlisle, PA: The Banner of Truth, 2009), p. 34.

it became clear to King David that he was the rich man who had deprived a poor man of his little ewe, his call did not change.

However, when King Ahab killed one of his citizens, Naboth, to possess his vineyard (1 Kings 21), the response of this king to his crimes was quite different compared to David's. The Lord sent the prophet Elijah the Tishbite to reprimand King Ahab. This prophet did not have time for parables and went straight to give his message:

> "This is what the Lord says: Have you murdered
> and also taken possession?" Ahab said to Elijah,
> "So, my enemy, you have found me, have you?"
> (1 Kings 21:19–20 CSB)

The prophet was his enemy. In the Edo dialect, *Ai gbi kor* means "you do not beat the messenger." There is no record of remorse or repentance on Ahab's part.

> Still, there was no one like Ahab, who devoted
> himself to do what was evil in the Lord's sight. (1
> Kings 21:25 CSB)

Repentance is an act of the heart or spirit, not an outward rending of clothes or appearance that simulates penance. Any acts of repentance Ahab had put up were to fulfill the law and dramatize the rituals of penance.

King Ahab was unable to acknowledge his sins and he continued to do evil in the Lord's sight. Yet he had exhibited the outward manifestations of contrition and penance—superficial repentance. In Nigerian parlance, this is "crocodile tears"— fake sorrow. "Look at me, I am doing it." Ahab tore his clothes, fasted, and put on sackcloth, but his heart was not repentant. "He committed the most detestable acts by following idols" (1 Kings 21:26 CSB).

Another significant factor of repentance is remorse. Sincere remorse for violating God's rule triggers regret and shame. There is an expression of sorrow motivated by the impact of offensive act—sorrow and tears driven by regret for having offended God. Tears that are driven by a deep heartfelt pain for error committed must be distinguished from Ahab's superficial expression of remorse.

Saint Paul presents the characteristics of sorrowing in a godly manner this way:

> I now rejoice, not because you were grieved, but because **your grief led to repentance**. For you were grieved as God willed, so that you didn't experience any loss from us. For **godly grief produces a repentance that leads to salvation** without regret, but worldly grief produces death. For consider how much diligence this very thing— this grieving as God wills—has produced in you: what a desire to clear yourselves, what indignation, what fear, what deep longing, what zeal,—what justice! In every way you showed yourselves to be pure in this matter. (2 Corinthians 7:9–12 CSB; emphasis mine)

Sincere remorse and grief for an offense result in repentance that leads to salvation that is fulfilling and without regret. However, "worldly grief produces death"—a separation from God. Sincere remorse produces a sense of diligence and authenticity, a desire to vindicate oneself from wrongdoing, and hatred for sin and doing wrong. Godly sorrow makes us hate committing sin. Essentially, this kind of sorrowing displaces sin from our lives. It does not say it makes us hate those who commit sin. It keeps us from sin. Hating those who commit abortion does not make you hate committing some other sin. We must first abhor sin in ourselves before we can condemn it in others. The ease with which we spy the sins of others makes it difficult for us to concede to our own sins.

Repentance is a strange concept to those who are unable to condemn wrongdoing or manifest shame. A culture that does not acknowledge shameful acts and pathologizes shame will be unable to acknowledge sinful acts. As Thomas Watson observed in *Doctrine of Repentance*, "There is no creature capable of shame but man. The brute beasts are capable of fear and pain, but not of shame. You cannot make a beast blush. Those who cannot blush for sin do too much resemble the beasts."[21]

Hatred for sin must be universal - hatred for all that displeases God, with all our faculties, in cognition, affection, and action. Our thought process must detest sinful ideas, our emotions and feelings must object to sin, and our behavior reflect our aversion to sin. Any and all sin contaminates us spiritually; hence abhorrence of sin must be against all forms of sin.

Godly sorrow induces fear of offending God and a longing to do what is right and just all the time. We become zealous about equity and justice, as every act of offense becomes repugnant to us. The sorrow of true repentance produces joy—the joy of salvation. King Ahab's kind of repentance seeks to fulfill the law with a show of the signs of contrition and penance. But repentance is an act of the heart in which, again in the words of Thomas Watson, "a sinner is inwardly humbled and visibly reformed."

> On the day of Pentecost after the people had heard Peter's sermon, they were pierced to the heart and said to Peter and the rest of the apostles, "Brothers, what should we do?" Peter replied, "**Repent and be baptized**, each of you, in the name of Jesus Christ **for the forgiveness of your sins**, and you

---

[21] Watson, *Doctrine of Repentance*, p. .

will receive the gift of the Holy Spirit." (Acts 2:37–38 CSB; emphasis mine)

When the people heard Peter's sermon they were "pierced to the heart." The piercing of the heart was followed by the instruction for all to "repent and be baptized…for the forgiveness of your sins." This order and sequence of events does not change. Speaking in tongues was not all that happened on the day of Pentecost. People repented and were baptized for the forgiveness of sin. This is the Good News.

Confession is an ingredient of repentance. The thorny question here is to whom we confess our sins. Think of King David again. Here is a summary of the verdict against him:

> Nathan replied to David, "You are the man! This is what the Lord God of Israel says: 'I anointed you king over Israel, and I rescued you from Saul. I gave your master's house to you and your master's into your arms, and I gave you the house of Israel and Judah, and if that was not enough, I would have given you even more. Why then have you despised the Lord's command by doing what I consider evil? You struck down Uriah the Hethite with the sword and took his wife as your own wife—you murdered him with the Ammonite's sword.'" (2 Samuel 12:7–9 CSB)

It can easily be argued that David misused his power and wronged Uriah by violating his wife. He also offended the woman he violated. For completeness, David stayed home to leisure instead of being at the front during wartime, and in so doing he offended the nation. David's response to Nathan in verse 13 underscores his state of mind: "I have sinned against the Lord" (2 Samuel 12:13 CSB). And in his repentance hymn he acknowledges, "Against you—you alone—I have sinned and done this evil in your sight" (Psalm 51:4a CSB).

The point is this: we apologize to the person whom we have offended, not through a third party. All sin is against God. And God's verdict is what matters and what is important. Think again of David saying, "I have sinned against the Lord." God, and God alone, was offended. Do you still wonder why David was the man after God's heart?

Our confession should be to God. Confessing our sins to fellow human beings may have the value of setting others up as persons to hold us accountable and help keep us from slipping back into sin. But that another human being can declare our sins forgiven is fallacy.

The parable of the Pharisee and the tax collector teaches us how to confess our sins and to whom.

> He also told this parable to some who trusted in themselves that they were righteous and looked down on everyone else: "Two men went up to the temple to pray, one a Pharisee and the other a tax collector. The Pharisee was standing and praying like this about himself: 'God, I thank you that I'm not like other people—greedy, unrighteous, adulterers, or even like this tax collector. I fast twice a week; I give a tenth of everything I get.' But the tax collector, standing far off, would not even raise his eyes to heaven but kept striking his chest and saying, 'God, have mercy on me, a sinner!'" (Luke 18:9–13 CSB)

When John wrote about confessing our sins to one another, he did not reference repentance.

Is anyone among you sick? He should call for
the elders of the church, and they are to pray
over him, anointing him with oil in the name
of the Lord. The prayer of faith will save the sick
person, and the Lord will raise him up; if he has
committed sins, he will be forgiven. Therefore,
confess your sins to one another and pray for one
another, so that you may be healed. The prayer
of a righteous person is very powerful in its effect.
(James 5:13–16 CSB)

Confessing our sins to one another is not for granting forgiveness
unto repentance but "that you may be healed."

Confession that is a component of repentance must be to
specific sins. However, confessing to a single act does not cover
for a pattern of behavior, just as admitting to telling a lie is not
admitting to being a liar. Confessing by using hyperboles and
exaggerating self-worth does not admit to being narcissistic or
a prideful person. Reframing our sinful acts in culturally and
socially acceptable language only satisfies man. God sees the
heart.

The following passage sets an example for confessing to the
specifics of an offense, and the confession was made to the Lord:

While Ezra prayed and confessed, weeping and
falling facedown before the house of God, an
extremely large assembly of Israelite men, women,
and children gathered around him. The people
also wept bitterly. Then Shecaniah son of Jehiel,
an Elamite, responded to Ezra, "We have been
unfaithful to our God by marrying foreign women
from the surrounding peoples, but there is still
hope for Israel in spite of this. Therefore, let's make
a covenant before our God to send away all the

foreign wives and their children, according to the counsel of my lord and of those who tremble at the command of our God. Let it be done according to the law. Get up, for this matter is your responsibility, and we support you. Be strong and take action!" Then Ezra got up and made the leading priests, Levites, and all Israel take an oath to do what had been said; so they took the oath. Ezra then went from the house of God and walked to the chamber of Jehohanan son of Eliashib, where he spent the night. He did not eat food or drink water, because he was mourning over the unfaithfulness of the exiles. They circulated a proclamation throughout Judah and Jerusalem that all the exiles should gather at Jerusalem. Whoever did not come within three days would forfeit all his possessions, according to the decision of the leaders and elders, and would be excluded from the assembly of the exiles. So all the men of Judah and Benjamin gathered in Jerusalem within the three days. On the twentieth day of the ninth month, all the people sat in the square at the house of God, trembling because of this matter and because of the heavy rain. Then the priest Ezra stood up and said to them, "You have been unfaithful by marrying foreign women, adding to Israel's guilt. Therefore, make a confession to the Lord, the God of your ancestors, and do his will. Separate yourselves from the surrounding peoples and your foreign wives." (Ezra 10:1–11 CSB)

If we confess our sins, he is faithful and righteous to forgive us our sins and to cleanse us from all unrighteousness. (1 John 1:8–9 CSB).

If we confess our sins to Him who can forgive them, He is the one who is faithful, He is the one who is righteous, and He is the one who will forgive. A person cannot deputize in this function.

The parable of the lost or prodigal son (Luke 15) is the flagship story of true repentance. The wasteful and extravagant son woke up one day and came to his senses. In the words of Jesus,

> "When he came to his senses, he said, 'How many of my father's hired workers have more than enough food, and here I am dying of hunger! I'll get up, go to my father, and say to him, "Father, I have sinned against heaven and in your sight. I'm no longer worthy to be called your son. Make me like one of your hired workers."' So he got up and went to his father. But while the son was still a long way off, his father saw him and was filled with compassion. He ran, threw his arms around his neck, and kissed him. The son said to him, 'Father, I have sinned against heaven and in your sight. I'm no longer worthy to be called your son.'" (Luke 15:17–21 CSB).

He acknowledged to himself what he was missing by rebelling and leaving home. He acknowledged he had a father ("How many of my father's hired workers"). He was prodigal but still a son. He was willing to admit that he had erred. He was not coerced into admitting his errors.

Like David, the prodigal son's transgressions were against heaven but in his father's sight: "Father, I have sinned against heaven and in your sight" (Luke 15:18). Like the tax collector, he felt unworthy and shameful for offending his father: "I'm no longer worthy to be called your son. Make me like one of your hired workers" (15:19 CSB).

Jesus here identified that we might feel offended by our

neighbor. Truly, it is God who is offended when we sin. We are only witnesses to the transgression. True heartfelt contrition is not colored with looks to draw attention.

Finally, repentance requires a commitment to turn away from sin and not to reoffend. A permanence in turning away from sin is necessary. True repentance calls for an action plan that is both in the past tense ("I repented") and continuing in the present tense ("I repent"). Repentance may have a starting point, but to be effective, it is an action that does not remain in the past.

Ezekiel tells us to turn from our idols and detestable ways that separate us from God. The Lord instructs him:

> "Therefore, say to the house of Israel, 'This is what the Lord God says: Repent and turn away from your idols; turn your faces away from all your detestable things. For when anyone from the house of Israel or from the aliens who reside in Israel separates himself from me, setting up idols in his heart and putting his sinful stumbling block in front of himself, and then comes to the prophet to inquire of me, I, the Lord, will answer him myself.'" (Ezekiel 14:6–7 CSB).

Repentance does not call for a one-time action; it demands abandoning, giving up completely and forsaking evil ways. "Let the wicked one abandon his way and the sinful one his thoughts; let him return to the Lord" (Isaiah 55:7a CSB).

Thomas Watson puts it this way:

> Dying to sin is the life of repentance. The very day a Christian turn from sin he must enjoin himself a perpetual fast. The eye must fast from impure glances. The ear must fast from hearing slanders. The tongue must fast from oaths. The hands must

fast from bribes. The feet must fast from the path of the harlot. And the soul must fast from the love of wickedness. This turning from sin implies a notable change.[22]

This requirement of repentance to be turned away from sin on a perpetual basis is the challenge for us all. And it is not a change of behavior, like making sure we are not arrested after committing a crime or making a New Year's Eve resolution. We must seek to turn from sin because God hates sin and because we desire to seek His face. If the scriptures call it a sin, we must have the conviction to turn from it. Reframing a sinful act as a culturally acceptable orientation or normative behavior does not change what it is.

A book by Robert W. Lee is my first time of seeing a book's title say so much all by itself: *A Sin by Any Other Name*.[23] A sin remains a sin regardless of how it is reframed or renamed. It remains repugnant to God no matter how we rearrange it for our convenience. Sinful acts are now conveniently sanitized and repackaged as crimes that a legal system may or may not punish. We deny that the hatred we harbor against each other does not offend God. They are just crimes against the country at the worst. Anyone could wield a weapon and flagrantly take the life of another and get away with it when they are of the right color, race, tribe, or religion. The Church remains silent. A deafening silence.

> Ezekiel again quotes the words of the Lord as delivered to him: "Tell them, 'As I live—this is the declaration of the Lord God—I take no pleasure in the death of the wicked, but rather that the wicked person should turn from his way and live.

---

[22] Watson, *Doctrine of Repentance*, p. .
[23] Robert W. Lee, *A Sin by Any Other Name*, (New York, Convergent Books: 2019).

Repent, repent of your evil ways! Why will you
die, house of Israel?'" (Ezekiel 33:11 CSB)

The desire to turn from sin must not come from the fear
of punishment or a desire for gain but primarily from love and
respect for the Supreme Being, God. In the Acts of Apostles, Paul
tells the Ephesians, "I testified to both Jews and Greeks about
repentance toward God and faith in our Lord Jesus" (Acts 20:21
CSB). And later:

> Instead, I preached to those in Damascus first,
> and to those in Jerusalem and in all the region
> of Judea, and to the Gentiles, that they should
> repent and turn to God, and do works worthy of
> repentance. (Acts 26:20 CSB)

The Lord lamented the sins of Ephraim and Judah through
the prophet Hosea. Their love for God's word was not sincere, the
covenant with God was violated, and God explained His feeling
of being betrayed.

> "For I desire faithful love and not sacrifice, the
> knowledge of God rather than burnt offerings.
> But they, like Adam, have violated the covenant;
> there they have betrayed me." (Hosea 6:67 CSB).

Just like today, the people rebelled and fled from the Lord. There
was turning, but not to God: "They turn, but not to what is above"
(Hosea 7:16a CSB).

Part of King Solomon's prayer while dedicating the Temple
of the Lord asked for forgiveness of the sins of the people, but he
did not just request that God forgive the people's sins. His prayer
recognized a process by means of which God will listen and hear
the petition of His people and forgive their sins: they will come

to their senses, repent, acknowledging they have sinned and done wrong, and then return to God, according to these conditions and steps:

> When they sin against you—for there is no one who does not sin—and you are angry with them and hand them over to the enemy, and their captors deport them to a distant or nearby country, and **when they come to their senses** in the land where they were deported and **repent** and petition you in their captors' land, **saying, "We have sinned and done wrong; we have been wicked,"** and **when they return** to you with all their mind and all their heart. (2 Chronicles 6:36–38 CSB; emphasis mine)

Second Chronicles 7:14 is often referenced to point out the fact that God is ready to forgive our sins and heal the land:

> "[When] my people, who bear my name, **humble themselves, pray and seek my face, and turn from their evil ways,** then I will hear from heaven, forgive their sin, and heal their land." (emphasis mine)

But the first part of this verse is often taken for granted. First, the verse is addressed to believers—"my people who are called by name"—not unbelievers. And then three conditions are prescribed: they are to humble themselves, pray and seek God's face, and then—the big one—turn from sinning. Only "then" will God hear and forgive our sins and heal us. Seeking God's forgiveness sincerely requires meeting all these requirements.

The lost son's father did not go out to seek the son. We might assume that since he was a man of wealth, he had the means to monitor his son's whereabouts and to know that the son had run out of money and was feeding out of a pigs' trough. It was not until the son met the conditions outlined above—came to his senses, acknowledged to himself that he had done wrong, convicted himself of the charges against him with due punishment to be a servant at his father's house, and then set out to face judgment— that the father demonstrated his grace and compassion for the son.

It used to be that the proverbial church mouse was poor. The priest and church leadership would not accept your offering when your source of income was unknown or suspicious. Pastors preached integrity to the congregation. But not now, at a time when looting the national treasury by senators and members of the House of Representatives is open knowledge, even fashionable. The church looks the other way and accepts the building of cathedrals and handsome donations, with which our reverends buy luxurious cars and jets and build themselves mansions and universities where church members cannot afford to send their children. The conscience of the nation dies, the salt loses its taste, and the people suffer when a nation lacks a prophet Nathan to speak truth to power. The church is compromised, and there is an urgent need to turn from the evil that has taken over the land.

There was a time when to be called a "tribalist" was insulting and shameful. To lift someone to the level of arch-tribalist was to call the person a devil. Today, pastors spew tribal hatred and anarchism from the pulpit while pointing the people to sowing seeds in the kingdom and exploiting their lack of knowledge and poverty. The church has failed to provide vision, nor is it able to lead the people to repent of their sins.

Thomas Watson calls the gospel of repentance

> a grace of God's Spirit whereby a sinner is inwardly humbled and visibly reformed. For a further amplification, know that repentance is a spiritual medicine made up of six special ingredients:

1. Sight of sin
2. Sorrow for sin
3. Confession of sin
4. Shame for sin
5. Hatred for sin
6. Turning from sin.

If any one is left out it loses its virtue.[24]

He went on to clarify that repentance is not fear of the consequence of guilt or "legal terror":

> Ahab and Judas had some trouble of mind. It is one thing to be a terrified sinner and another to be a repenting sinner. Sense of guilt is enough to breed terror. Repentance depends upon a change of heart. There may be terror, yet with no change of heart.

Nor is repentance the declaration of resolutions and vows not to sin. Resolutions are often made for fear of the painful consequences of sin and "not because sin is sinful." Nor is it repentance when the reasons for leaving sinful acts derive from personal convenience and not from reception of God's grace. "Sin may be parted with, yet without repentance."

---

[24] Watson, *Doctrine of Repentance*, p.18

CHAPTER 7

WHAT ABOUT GRACE?

The word "grace" is used several times in the scriptures. Unlike the term "faith," grace is not explicitly defined. The concept of grace and the use of the word have hence acquired multiple interpretations and expressions. Hebrews 11:1 explicitly states what faith is: "Now faith is the reality of what is hoped for, the proof of what is not seen." And chapter 11 is devoted in its entirety to those who believed and for whom it was counted as righteousness. *Collins English Dictionary* defines the noun *grace* as "elegance or beauty of form, manner, motion, or action." And as a verb, *grace* is defined as "do honor or credit to (someone or something) by one's presence." As a concept in the scripture, the common definition of *grace* is "the unmerited favor of God towards us." This definition seems not to consider that grace is often used in the context of "the grace of God." Grace, therefore, is a quality of God, one of His attributes or characteristics—hence the phrase "the grace of God":

> Make sure that no one falls short of **the grace of God** and that no root of bitterness springs up, causing trouble and defiling many. (Hebrews 12:15 CSB; emphasis mine)

The favors we get because of this quality of God is not what grace is. The favors we get because of God's grace are the *manifestations* of His grace, the manifestations of this characteristic of His. Grace is the quality of God that makes Him love us despite ourselves. God is holy, omnipotent, omnipresent, and all-powerful. He is also gracious.

The prophet Jonah got instruction from God to go to Nineveh and preach to the people of Nineveh that their evil was about to draw the wrath of God. Jonah chose not to go on this errand. He got himself a ticket and headed in the opposite direction from Nineveh on a ship. A great storm came upon the ship. When the ship's captain, crew, and other passengers confronted Jonah, the following exchange took place:

> He answered them, "I'm a Hebrew. I worship the Lord, the God of the heavens, who made the sea and the dry land." Then the men were seized by a great fear and said to him, "What have you done?" The men knew he was fleeing from the Lord's presence because he had told them. So they said to him, "What should we do to you so that the sea will calm down for us?" For the sea was getting worse and worse. He answered them, "Pick me up and throw me into the sea so that it will calm down for you, for I know that I'm to blame for this great storm that is against you." (Jonah 1:9–12 CSB)

Jonah chose to commit suicide rather than turn round and fulfill his errand. He had no plans to survive when he asked to be thrown into the storm. He was not going to obey God—period.

Or so he thought. However, Jonah was delivered to Nineveh, and God spoke to him a second time. This time Jonah went about Nineveh and preached as he had been instructed to. And to his surprise, the people of Nineveh turned from their evil ways—repented—and God did not visit them with the disaster He had threatened.

That the Ninevites got pardon and escaped God's punishment greatly displeased and angered Jonah. He shared his mind with God:

> "Please, Lord, isn't this what I said while I was still in my own country? That's why I fled toward Tarshish in the first place. I knew that you are a gracious and compassionate God, slow to anger, abounding in faithful love, and one who relents from sending disaster." (Jonah 4:2 CSB)

God did not give the Ninevites grace or favor. His love for the sinner was manifested through His grace. God did not give Jonah grace or favor; He exhibited His graceful nature: "I knew that you are gracious." Jonah got a waiver on his disobedience because there seemed to be a purpose, an assignment only he could fulfill. Often, God's grace confers a purpose on the recipient.

In the book of Genesis, Abram is introduced as the son of Terah, brother to Nahor and Haran, and Sarai's husband (11:26–29). The next thing is that Abram is taking God's orders and blessings. There is no information on why God picked Abram for the blessings poured on him. Apparently, God had maintained a one-sided relationship with Abram that did not depend on Abram's performance but rather on God's grace—God's ability to relate with us despite ourselves—a one-sided contract. Other than that He wanted to, there is no other reason God entered a threefold contract with Abram. Abram was only expected to follow God's direction to a chosen place. Just come and "I will," the contract states.

The Lord said to Abram:
"Go from your land,
your relatives,
and your father's house
to the land that **I will** show you.
I will make you into a great nation,
I will bless you,
I will make your name great,
and you will be a blessing.
I will bless those who bless you,
I will curse anyone who treats you with contempt,
and all the peoples on earth
will be blessed through you." (Genesis 12:1–3
CSB; emphasis mine)

For Abram, his part of this arrangement was easy. He got up, took his wife and other relatives and possessions, and did what he was asked to do: go find a land the Lord would show him. Abram believed that God would execute this one-sided agreement if he relocated. No questions asked. His age and his wife's age were not relevant. Faith!

God appeared to Abram in a dream a second time, apparently to address Abram's unspoken concerns about God's side of this contract as expressed by the multiple "I will."

After these events, the word of the Lord came to Abram in a vision: "Do not be afraid, Abram. I am your shield; your reward will be very great." (Genesis 15:1 CSB)

Abram's belief that God would do what He said He would do earned him an extra credit: righteousness. "Abram believed the Lord, and He credited it to him as righteousness" (Genesis 15:6 CSB)

Noah believed God and built an ark in anticipation of a flood. But in God's relationship with Abram, credit was awarded for this undoubting trust in God. As Andy Stanley in *The Grace of God* aptly put it, "In Abraham, God established the relational ground rule for all mankind: **a right standing with God comes through faith in the promises of God.**"[25] Stanley goes on,

> In response to Abram's faith, God declared him righteous (v. 6). God said, in effect, "Because you have trusted in me, I give you the gift of righteousness. I have written forgiveness across your moral ledger sheet. Because of your faith, I have cleared your account of all debt." **At that very moment, the Lord established an important precedent: a righteous standing with God comes through faith.** This is the single most important aspect of God's grace.[26]

To the faithful, God does forgive sins without repentance when He displays the magnitude of His grace. The two sides of the narrow gate of salvation are believing in the Son of God (faith) and repentance. Both conditions are mandatory. It is not either/or, but both. But because of His grace, God does grant us forgiveness and righteousness when we have undoubting belief and trust in His power. Before the throne of God's grace, there is mercy, compassion, the gift of righteousness, forgiveness, and love.

In the letter to the Ephesians, Paul writes, "For you are saved by grace through faith, and this is not from yourselves; it is God's gift—not from works, so that no one can boast" (Ephesians 2:89 CSB). The apostle to the Gentiles is saying that we are saved because of God's grace when we believe in Him—when we

---

[25] Andy Stanley, *The Grace of God*, (Nashville, TN: Thomas Nelson, 2010), p. 30.

[26] Stanley, *The Grace of God*, pp. 24–25, (emphases as in the original).

have faith. Abraham believed and the record was made of God manifesting His grace. Beyond trusting and believing, Abraham had no other works to earn him righteousness and salvation.

The apostle Paul, known earlier in his life as Saul, knew much about being on the receiving end of God's grace. When he is introduced as Saul in the Acts of Apostles, he seems to have had a supervisory role in the martyrdom of Saint Stephen, standing by and monitoring the stoning of Stephen. He agreed or approved of putting him to death (Acts 8:1). Those who did the actual stoning and killing of Stephen laid their garments at the feet of Saul. After this initial success at executing a believer, Saul was emboldened and went on a rampage, searching from house to house for believers to put in prison.

> They dragged him out of the city and began to stone him. And the witnesses laid their garments at the feet of a young man named Saul. (Acts 7:58 CSB)

> Saul, however, was ravaging the church. He would enter house after house, drag off men and women and put them in prison. (Acts 8:3 CSB)

Saul sought and obtained letters of commendation and authority to travel to cities and to torment followers of Christ. On his way to Damascus and with his execution letter at hand, he was confronted.

> Now Saul was still breathing threats and murder against the disciples of the Lord. He went to the high priest and requested letters from him to the synagogues in Damascus, so that if he found any men or women who belonged to the Way, he might bring them as prisoners to Jerusalem. As he

traveled and was nearing Damascus, a light from heaven suddenly flashed around him. Falling to the ground, he heard a voice saying to him, "Saul, Saul, why are you persecuting me?" "Who are you, Lord?" Saul said. "I am Jesus, the one you are persecuting," he replied. "But get up and go into the city, and **you will be told what you must do**." The men who were traveling with him stood speechless, hearing the sound but seeing no one. Saul got up from the ground, and though his eyes were open, he could see nothing. So they took him by the hand and led him into Damascus. He was unable to see for three days and did not eat or drink. (Acts 9:1–9 CSB; emphasis mine)

Saul persecuted those who followed the Way until he was stopped en route to Damascus on a mission against believers. Saul had no alignment with Jesus. But God's grace shone on him and gave him an assignment.

Grace is a quality of God that reflects His ability to overlook our sins and use us as His vessel. God's grace confers a purpose, a calling to an assignment which is often difficult to avoid. "Get up and go into the city, and you will be told what you must do"—yes, *must* do! Under God's grace, we receive a waiver on repentance and obtain forgiveness but get a new purpose, an assignment in His vineyard.

In his first epistle to the Corinthians, Paul had occasion to testify about God's grace in his life.

For I am the least of the apostles, not worthy to be called an apostle, because I persecuted the church of God. But by the grace of God, I am what I am, and his grace toward me was not in vain. On the contrary, I worked harder than any of them, yet

not I, but the grace of God that was with me. (1
Corinthians 15:9–10 CSB)

To the Galatians, Paul wrote:

> For you have heard about my former way of life in
> Judaism: I intensely persecuted God's church and
> tried to destroy it. I advanced in Judaism beyond
> many contemporaries among my people, because
> I was extremely zealous for the traditions of my
> ancestors. But when God, who from my mother's
> womb set me apart and **called me by his grace**,
> was pleased to reveal his Son in me, **so that I
> could preach him among the Gentiles,** I did
> not immediately consult with anyone. (Galatians
> 1:13–16 CSB; emphasis mine)

Are we then to live in sin so that as believers we will obtain
forgiveness without repentance because of God's grace? Is baptism
unto repentance undermined? Paul says "No!" How can the
believer who has died to sin at baptism continue in sin? Should
sin then abound so that Grace will multiply? No!

> What should we say then? Should we continue
> in sin so that grace may multiply? Absolutely
> not! How can we who died to sin still live in it?
> (Romans 6:1–2 CSB)

In his first letter to Timothy, Paul gives testimony that he had
received strength through Jesus Christ, who had appointed him
into His ministry. Paul confessed to being the worst of sinners,
who was saved to demonstrate God's patience with sinners who
will believe. Paul recounts that his salvation came out of God's
mercy and an overflow of grace.

I give thanks to Christ Jesus our Lord who has strengthened me, because he considered me faithful, appointing me to the ministry—even though I was formerly a blasphemer, a persecutor, and an arrogant man. But I received mercy because I acted out of ignorance in unbelief, and the grace of our Lord overflowed, along with the faith and love that are in Christ Jesus. This saying is trustworthy and deserving of full acceptance: "Christ Jesus came into the world to save sinners"—and I am the worst of them. But I received mercy for this reason, so that in me, the worst of them, Christ Jesus might demonstrate his extraordinary patience as an example to those who would believe in him for eternal life. (1 Timothy 1:12–16 CSB)

The grace of God is not a favor or gift of God; it is a quality that God exudes, a character that only He exhibits. When this behavior is directed at us, we get forgiveness of our sins and an appointment to an assignment. Grace flows from gracious God with consequences.

Paul, the apostle commissioned to preach "baptism to repentance for the forgiveness of sins" to Gentiles (everyone but Jews), never had occasion to repent of his past. He was stopped in his tracks, redirected, and given his assignment. Paul seems to have had a struggle with his exemption and waiver from repenting and yet having been elevated to the status of an apostle. His internal struggle constituted "a thorn in his flesh."

In his second letter to the Corinthians, Paul acknowledged that the grief he caused the Corinthians in a prior letter was worth it because the grief produced repentance, a genuine repentance that led to salvation. Paul, who had a waiver on repentance because of God's grace, is causing others to repent.

For even if I grieved you with my letter, I don't regret it. And if I regretted it—since I saw that the letter grieved you, yet only for a while—I now rejoice, not because you were grieved, but because **your grief led to repentance**. For you were grieved as God willed, so that you didn't experience any loss from us. For godly grief produces **a repentance that leads to salvation** without regret, but worldly grief produces death. (2 Corinthians 7:8–10 CSB; emphasis mine)

For most of the rest of Second Corinthians, Paul seems to be responding to detractors he called "false prophets" (11:13). He recounted his qualifications to preach Christ and how much suffering and pain he had been through to preach the Gospel of Christ. He will not boast,

for if I want to boast, I wouldn't be a fool, because I would be telling the truth. But I will spare you, so that no one can credit me with something beyond what he sees in me or hears from me, especially because of the extraordinary revelations. Therefore, so that I would not exalt myself, a thorn in the flesh was given to me, a messenger of Satan to torment me so that I would not exalt myself. Concerning this, I pleaded with the Lord three times that it would leave me. But he said to me, "My grace is sufficient for you, for my power is perfected in weakness." (2 Corinthians 12:6–9 CSB)

Those he called false prophets who are messengers of Satan were tormenting him and disparaging him. The apparent contradiction that Saul, the persecutor of Christians, could be preaching for

Christ became a concern for the apostle. Paul seems to have taken his worries to God in prayers three times. And all three times Paul was reassured that he was called, and God's grace should be enough for him.

The "thorn in my flesh" that Paul spoke of could well be a physical ailment. The response he got having taken the thorn to the Lord suggests that the thorn may well have been a spiritual concern: his ministry under attack. Hence the reassurance from the Lord, "My grace is sufficient for you."

In chapter 8 of his letter to the Romans, Paul seems to take a direct swing at his detractors. He wonders how anyone could find fault with one God has chosen. He goes on to affirm that nothing will make him lose the love of God he has been called into. He affirmed that no amount of persecution will make him rebel and be disobedient against God again. In Romans 8:37–38, Paul is saying that nothing will make him ever sin against God again. Under grace, we must strive not to sin again, because sin does separates us from the love of God.

> Who can bring an accusation against God's elect? God is the one who justifies. Who is the one who condemns? Christ Jesus is the one who died, but even more, has been raised; he also is at the right hand of God and intercedes for us. Who can separate us from the love of Christ? Can affliction or distress or persecution or famine or nakedness or danger or sword? (Romans 8:33–35 CSB)

The rhetorical questions in these verses suggest the struggle Paul was going through. Who can accuse someone whom God Himself has elected? Who is qualified to condemn? Only Christ Jesus!

Paul had experienced the love of God through His Grace and could not imagine what can make him lose this love. First John 4:7 declares "God is love." And John 3:16 amplifies His demonstration of His loving nature towards us. He so loved us that "He gave," as an act of sacrificing, His Son for us. This same God who loves us so passionately and is gracious towards us equally abhors and detests sin. In Romans 8:33–35, Paul is affirming and declaring that no temptation by way of persecution, punishment, torture, or criticism will make him sin and loose the love of God. In Romans 11:22, he draws attention to the fact that Jonah's gracious and compassionate God also has a severe side. God is good—all the time. God equally, and intensely, abhors sin all the time. God's goodness towards us is not sustained when we remain in disobedience.

> Therefore, consider God's kindness and severity: severity toward those who have fallen but God's kindness toward you—if you remain in his kindness. Otherwise you too will be cut off. (Romans 11:22 CSB)

Christians are segregated by denominations and creed. Even within the same denomination, we most often are segregated by skin color, race, ethnicity, and nationality. A person of color takes over a church as minister, and all others who are not of that race exit the church. How do we reciprocate and demonstrate God's love in us?

> Dear friends, let us love one another, because love is from God, and everyone who loves has been born of God and knows God. The one who does not love does not know God, because God is love. God's love was revealed among us in this way: God sent his one and only Son into the world so that we might live through him. Love consists in this: not that we loved God, but that he loved

us and sent his Son to be the atoning sacrifice for our sins. (1 John 4:7–10 CSB)

We love because he first loved us. If anyone says, "I love God," and yet hates his brother or sister, he is a liar. For the person who does not love his brother or sister whom he has seen cannot love God whom he has not seen. And we have this command from him: The one who loves God must also love his brother and sister. (1 John 4:19– 21 CSB)

Is God's love for us reciprocated through our love for one another? Is it lip service? Does grace exempt us from this condition? God is love, God is gracious, yet God abhors and punishes sin. It is difficult to state this better than Andy Stanley: "The fact is, God is both terrifying and merciful. God hates evil and he loves people. **God punishes sin and he extends grace to sinners.**"[27]

The sinner on the receiving end of God's grace often has an assignment, a purpose for having their sins covered. Blessed is the person whose evil deeds are not recorded against them.

Blessed are those whose lawless acts are forgiven
and whose sins are covered.
Blessed is the person
the Lord will never charge with sin. (Romans 4:7–8 CSB)
How joyful is the one
whose transgression is forgiven, whose sin is covered!
How joyful is a person whom
the Lord does not charge with iniquity
and in whose spirit is no deceit! (Psalm 32:1–2 CSB)

---

[27] Stanley, *The Grace of God*, p. 78, (emphasis in original).

Before Saul, who later became Paul, there was Rahab the prostitute. In the second chapter of Joshua, Rahab is introduced as a harlot. Not the greatest introduction for someone who saved the spies Joshua had sent to spy on Jericho! Rahab hid the two spies and lied to the king of Jericho to save the Israelite spies. Before releasing the spies to safety, Rahab stated what she had heard about the itinerant Jews. Her conclusions compelled her to seek a contract with the spies to the effect that when the Jews eventually conquered Jericho, she and her family would be spared.

> "When we heard this, we lost heart, and everyone's courage failed because of you, for the Lord your God is God in heaven above and on earth below. Now please swear to me by the Lord that you will also show kindness to my father's family, because I showed kindness to you. Give me a sure sign that you will spare the lives of my father, mother, brothers, sisters, and all who belong to them, and save us from death."

> The men answered her, "We will give our lives for yours. If you don't report our mission, we will show kindness and faithfulness to you when the Lord gives us the land." (Joshua 2:11–14 CSB)

Rahab had her contract executed positively. She and her family members, who took refuge in her house when the Israelites stormed Jericho, were saved. The Israelites fulfilled their side of the contract with Rahab as agreed. The agreement to save Rahab and her family did not reference her profession nor require a change of occupational status as precondition. Rahab was integrated into the Jewish community, and the next time she is mentioned in the scriptures, her name shows up in the genealogy of David, the son of Jesse. Grace elevates us out of sin and confers a purpose.

Grace repositioned the lying Canaanite prostitute in the lineage of the Savior.

> An account of the genealogy of Jesus Christ, the Son of David, the Son of Abraham: Abraham fathered Isaac, Isaac fathered Jacob, Jacob fathered Judah and his brothers, Judah fathered Perez and Zerah by Tamar, Perez fathered Hezron, Hezron fathered Aram, Aram fathered Amminadab, Amminadab fathered Nahshon, Nahshon fathered Salmon, **Salmon fathered Boaz by Rahab**, Boaz fathered Obed by Ruth, Obed fathered Jesse, and Jesse fathered King David. (Matthew 1:1–6 CSB; emphasis mine)

Grace is not coverage to continue a life in disobedience to God, apostatized by worshiping ourselves and other idols, resorting to false prophesy, lying and killing with our tongues, peddling "alternate truths," and reframing acts that displease God as a new dispensation. Grace creates an exemption from repentance and assigns a purpose that glorifies God. By grace, the lying Gentile prostitute Rahab was positioned in the lineage of Christ. By grace, Rahab got assigned a position of elevated favor in the incarnation of Christ.

When the woman at the well encountered Jesus, she too encountered grace. The encounter between Jesus and the unnamed Samaritan woman is often recounted because of Christ's request for water to drink and His offer of "living water" that stops all thirst. Beyond this, the Samaritan woman at the well had a review of her past unworthy life from the Master and instant conferment with a ministry of evangelism and power to call others to Christ. She encountered grace at the well and obtained a waiver on her sins and an assignment to bring others to Christ waiting at the well.

A woman of Samaria came to draw water. "Give me a drink," Jesus said to her, because his disciples had gone into town to buy food. "How is it that you, a Jew, ask for a drink from me, a Samaritan woman?" she asked him. "For Jews do not associate with Samaritans." Jesus answered, "If you knew the gift of God, and who is saying to you, 'Give me a drink,' you would ask him, and he would give you living water." (John 4:7–10 CSB)

Now many Samaritans from that town believed in him because of what the woman said when she testified, "He told me everything I ever did." So when the Samaritans came to him, they asked him to stay with them, and he stayed there two days. Many more believed because of what he said. And they told the woman, "We no longer believe because of what you said, since we have heard for ourselves and know that this really is the Savior of the world." (John 4:39–42 CSB)

Maybe the disciples who left Christ at the well to go into the same Sychar village ministered to those they bought food from and others they met on the road. The records do not say. But by grace, the ministry of a Gentile woman brought others to Christ and even caused Christ to delay two more days at Sychar. Grace calls us as we are to a purpose. Under grace, we cannot return to as we were. We cannot remain as we were and claim grace. Grace transforms and the struggle to remain under grace calls us to a life of repentance.

The scripture has many more instances of the manifestation of God's grace, and every time there is a purpose for the extension of grace to a sinner. And because we all sin, we all need God's grace for salvation.

"As it is written: There is no one righteous, not even one. There is no one who understands; there is no one who seeks God. All have turned away; all alike have become worthless. There is no one who does what is good, not even one. Their throat is an open grave; they deceive with their tongues. Vipers' venom is under their lips. Their mouth is full of cursing and bitterness. Their feet are swift to shed blood; ruin and wretchedness are in their paths, and the path of peace they have not known. There is no fear of God before their eyes. (Romans 3:10–18 CSB)

The righteousness of God is through faith in Jesus Christ to all who believe, since there is no distinction. For all have sinned and fall short of the glory of God. (Romans 3:22–23 CSB)

We do not all need Paul's experience with grace, or be recalcitrant and disobedient Jonah, or be a Rahab. We do not need to be the woman at the well who became an evangelist when she encountered grace. However, God's grace calls us all to repentance for the salvation of our souls. "I have not come to call the righteous, but sinners to repentance" (Luke 5:32 CSB).

"Therefore, house of Israel, I will judge each one of you according to his ways." This is the declaration of the Lord God. "**Repent and turn from all your rebellious acts**, so they will not become a sinful stumbling block to you. Throw off all the transgressions you have committed, and get yourselves a new heart and a new spirit. Why should you die, house of Israel? **For I take no pleasure in anyone's death.**" This is the declaration of the Lord God. So repent and live. (Ezekiel 18:30–32 CSB; emphasis mine)

CHAPTER 8

THE REWARD FOR REPENTANCE

When the decision was made to crucify Jesus along with criminals the intent was to cast Him as an offender. This was after Pilate stated, "I find no grounds for charging this man." (Luke 23:4 CSB)

E ssentially, Jesus was sentenced to death *after* being discharged for lack of charge and evidence.

If the scriptures and the prophecies related to Jesus had to be fulfilled, it was not up to Pilate. Prophet Isaiah had declared that the savoir will submit to dying among criminals, bear the sins of others, and forgive and intercede for the criminals.

> Therefore I will give him the many as a portion,
> and he will receive the mighty as spoil,
> because he willingly submitted to death,
> and was counted among the rebels;
> yet he bore the sin of many
> and interceded for the rebels. (Isaiah 53:12 CSB)

The Gospel of Luke three times records that Jesus referenced the prophecies about Him and affirmed that these predictions would be fulfilled. His disciples did not comprehend.

But he strictly warned and instructed them to tell this to no one, saying, "It is necessary that the Son of Man suffer many things and be rejected by the elders, chief priests, and scribes, be killed, and be raised the third day." (Luke 9:21–22 CSB)

Second,

"Let these words sink in: The Son of Man is about to be betrayed into the hands of men." But they did not understand this statement; it was concealed from them so that they could not grasp it, and they were afraid to ask him about it. (Luke 9:44–45 CSB)

And the third time He took the twelve aside and repeated that He was going to be assaulted, mocked, spat on, flogged, and killed.

"See, we are going up to Jerusalem. **Everything that is written through the prophets about the Son of Man will be accomplished.** For he will be handed over to the Gentiles, and he will be mocked, insulted, spit on; and after they flog him, they will kill him, and he will rise on the third day." (Luke 18:31–33 CSB; emphasis mine)

The Gospels of Matthew and Mark both have corresponding verses that record these three occasions when Jesus predicted His death (Matthew 16:21–23, 17:22–23, 20:17–19; Mark 8:31–33, 9:30–32, 10:32–34).

When the prophecies and His predictions came to fulfillment, Jesus also had occasion to model His message of repentance. He did not set the stage. He was set up to be humiliated as a rebel, a criminal, or thief. The scriptures were fulfilled, and Jesus had opportunity to demonstrate that His message of repentance had reward. When we remain defiant and or rationalize our sins, we remain condemned. However, when we acknowledge Him and repent of our wrongdoings, there is reward of salvation.

> When they arrived at the place called The Skull, they crucified him there, along with the criminals, one on the right and one on the left. (Luke 23:33 (CSB)

> There they crucified him and two others with him, one on either side, with Jesus in the middle. (John 19:18 CSB)

> Then one of the criminals hanging there began to yell insults at him: "Aren't you the Messiah? Save yourself and us!" But the other answered, rebuking him: "Don't you even fear God, since you are undergoing the same punishment? We are punished justly, because we're getting back what we deserve for the things we did, but this man has done nothing wrong." Then he said, "Jesus, remember me when you come into your kingdom." And he said to him, "Truly I tell you, today you will be with me in paradise." (Luke 23:39–43 CSB)

The plot to criminalize Jesus became an opportunity for Him, one last time, to expose the fact that repentance, the theme of His ministry on earth, carried a prize—the prize of salvation. And defiance, rationalizing our sins, seeking to be culturally and politically correct, leaves us condemned.

Choose you this day.

BIBLE REFERENCES

Preface
John 18:15–26, Luke 17:7–10, Galatians 3:10, Mark 6:12, Luke 24:46–47

Chapter 1. "Go and Sin No More": A Significant Condition for Salvation
Numbers 22:22–35, Exodus 20:7, Ezekiel 34:10, Matthew 11:28, John 8:3–11

Chapter 3. What is Forgiveness?
Luke 23:34a, Acts 7:57–60, Matthew18:23–35, Ephesians 4: 26–27, 31, 32, Matthew 18:21

Chapter 4. Repentance-Induced Forgiveness
Matt 6: 12, Jonah 4:2b, Psalms 103:3–14, Psalms 86:15, Hebrew 2:17, John 3:14–16, 3:36,
Matthew 4:17, Mark 1:4, 15, Luke 24: 46–47, Mark16:15–16, Matthew 7:21–22, Matthew 7:13–14, Romans 3:23, Luke 13:2–5, 1 John 1:8–10, Luke 5:32, Luke 15:11–31, Matthew 5:22a
Matthew 21:28–32, Matthew 11:20–2, Matthew 11:20–21

Chapter 5. What Is Sin? When Do We Need Forgiveness?
Genesis 3, Genesis 1:28, Genesis 2:16–17, Genesis 2:2–3, Ezekiel 18:2–4, Ezekiel 18:19–20
Genesis 4, Genesis 4:3–9,

Chapter 6. The Principles of Repentance

Luke 15:3–10, 1 King 8:46–50, Daniel 9:4–19; Psalm 38:18, Psalm 51:4, 2 Samuel, 11, 12, Psalm 15, 1 Kings 21, 2 Corinthians 7:9–12, Acts 2:37–38, 2 Samuel 12:7–9, 12–13, Psalms 51:4a, Luke 18:9–13, James 5:13–16, Ezra 10:1–11, 1 John 1:8–9, Ezekiel 14:6–7, Ezekiel 33:10–11, Acts 20:21, Acts 26:20, Hosea 6:6–7, Hosea 7:16a, 2 Chronicles 6:36–38, 2 Chronicles 7:14,

Chapter 7. What about Grace?

Hebrews 11:1, Hebrews 12:15, Jonah 1:9–12, Genesis 11:26–29, Genesis 12:1–3, Genesis 15:1
Genesis 15:6, Ephesians 2:8–9, Acts 8:1, Acts 7:58, Acts 8:3, 1 Corinthians 15:9–10, Galatians 1:13–16, Romans 6:1–2, 1 Timothy 1:12–16, 2 Corinthians 7:8–10, 2 Corinthians 12:6–9, Romans 8:37–38, Romans 8:33–35, 1 John 4:7, John 3:16, 1 John 4:7–10, 19–21, Romans 4:7–8, Psalms 32:1–2, Joshua 2:11–14, Matthew 1:1–6, John 4:7–10, John 4:39–42, Romans 3:10–18, Romans 3:22–23, Luke 5:32, Ezekiel 18:30–32,

Chapter 8. The Reward for Repentance

Luke 23:4; Isaiah 53:12; Luke 9:21–22; Luke 9:44–45; Luke 18:31–33; Luke 23:33; John 19:18; Luke 23:39–43

ABOUT THE AUTHOR

Osilama Osime, a retired medical practitioner, spent several years practicing tropical medicine in Sub-Sahara Africa. He is a student of the Bible and is particularly interested in the question of theodicy—or why God permits evil. He earned numerous degrees, including a Bachelor of Medicine and Bachelor of Surgery from the University of Benin, Benin City; a Master of Public Health from the Boston University School of Public Health; and a Master of Science from Salem State University in Salem, Massachusetts. He is married and has five grandchildren.